T0269938

BOCCONI
UNIVERSITY
PRESS

Mario Patrono · Arianna Vedaschi

DONALD TRUMP
AND THE FUTURE OF
AMERICAN DEMOCRACY

The Harbinger of a Storm?

Cover: Cristina Bernasconi, Milan
Typesetting: Laura Panigara, Cesano Boscone (MI)

Copyright © 2023 Bocconi University Press
EGEA S.p.A.

EGEA S.p.A.
Via Salasco, 5 - 20136 Milano
Tel. 02/5836.5751 – Fax 02/5836.5753
egea.edizioni@unibocconi.it – www.egeaeditore.it

First edition: March 2023

ISBN Domestic Edition	979-12-80623-06-5
ISBN Digital Domestic Edition	978-88-238-8590-5
ISBN International Edition	978-88-313-2276-8
ISBN Digital International Edition	978-88-313-2287-4

Print: Logo s.r.l., Borgoricco (PD)

Contents

Part Three
Some Potential Bolsters to Insert (or Restore)
in the American Democratic System

Part Four
The Constitution, Interpretation
of the Constitution, and Democracy

The present work takes into account facts and circumstances happened during, and not after, the Trump presidency.

The Authors would like to thank Dr. Chiara Graziani, Ph.D., for providing her research assistance during the steps aimed at writing this book.

Foreword

by *Tom Ginsburg*

In the 1990s, many of us in the United States watched developments in Italian politics with a mix of fascination and disbelief. After most of the political class was caught up in the *tangentopoli* scandal, a billionaire amateur politician who broke all the rules arrived to lead the country. Silvio Berlusconi went on to become the longest-serving Prime Minister in postwar Italian history, stabilizing a discredited system but also providing occasional moments of controversy and scandal.

What a difference a couple of decades makes. The 2016 election of our very own billionaire in the person of Donald Trump means that we are no longer entertained. Trump's distinctive presidency shredded many of the norms of American politics, and ended with a riot in the Capitol building that sought to interrupt the peaceful transfer of power. It is now ourselves that we look at with a mix of fascination and disbelief: whatever Berlusconi's misdeeds, they were marginal violations of norms rather than radical challenges to democratic rotation. What kind of country is this anyway? How could the world's oldest democracy elect and tolerate a leader with such thin commitments to that form of government?

One might forgive a certain *schadenfreude* on the part of any Italian scholar examining the United States in the aftermath of Trump. Yet in this book, Professors Mario Patrono and Arianna Vedaschi are not celebrating. Instead, they conduct a cool analysis of the situation, looking at the structural conditions that gave rise to the current threats to American democracy, and carefully evaluating their prospects for success. They see continuing trends that allowed Trump, an instinctive politician, to capitalize on racial resentments and activate new forces of reaction.

Like Alexis de Tocqueville nearly two centuries ago, their distance from the United States allows Patrono and Vedaschi to see things more clearly. The result is a book that is honest about the very real continuing threats, exacerbated by certain holes in the constitutional order of the United States. The authors show that a determined autocrat could manipulate the various lacunae and ambiguities in a two-hundred year old Constitution, but thankfully, they also identify many of the resources that remain in place to deter such a prospect. Many institutions remain strong, even if shrill and increasingly violent discourse causes much hand-wringing. The January 6 insurrection seems to have increased voter engagement, rather than reducing it. American constitutional politics remains a warzone, but hopefully only in the figurative sense.

It is often said that Italy is ahead of the curve when it comes to politics. Whether or not that turns out to be the case, we have in this book good evidence that Italian scholars are ahead of the curve when it comes to the analysis of constitutional democracy in our fraught era.

Part One
The Erosion of Liberal Democracy:
A Phenomenon that Concerns
the United States too?

1 Fukuyama's Prophecy and the Great Illusion

Whoever wants to understand the real dynamics underpinning democracy should give up the idea of thinking about it in the singular, except as an archetype or ideal model. In live politics, democracy does not work in the same way anywhere, but there are democracies working differently from each other in each individual country. If this is the case, then the very common phenomenon often defined as the "erosion" or the "eclipse" of democracy can have different causes in different systems. All these causes may have surfaced purely and simply by coincidence in our historical period. There are, however, three causes that hold true in general terms, or that anyway hold true in many cases. To understand what we are talking about, we need to climb into a "time machine" and travel back in time, about 30 years.

The abrupt collapse of a whole established order ensuing on the breakdown of the Communist Hemisphere (1989–1991) gave birth, in the West, to a Great Illusion. The world had ceased being a military arena with two opposing alternative and mutually incompatible social models, such that – and this was the Great Illusion – the values and institutions of the West would take the route to becoming the values and institutions of all mankind. In the field of political theory, this Great Illusion was proclaimed above all by the political scientist Francis Fukuyama. In a book that provoked lively cultural debate – *The End of History and the Last Man*, published in 1992[1] – he maintained that we had reached the Hegelian supremacy of the Spirit and were at the "end of History," since there was no alternative to the liberal democracy and capitalism of the Western tradition.

This Great Illusion lasted, it may well be said, from morning till night. In fact, it was almost immediately clear that the United States, theoretically to become "the linchpin of the hoped-for new world order"[2] and to play the role of "world police force," did not have sufficient strength to shoulder such a steady unipolar scenario.[3] The 9/11 cut a Great Wound in the very flesh of the American people. The vulnerability of the United States suddenly became visible to the eyes of the world in a tragic and spectacular way, and its decline, immersed in the cloud of dust raised by the collapse of the Twin Towers, had become a reality. The attack of jihadist terrorism that day intervened, laying the tombstone on the Great Illusion.

Fukuyama's prophecy – the planet-wide triumph of liberal democracy under the leadership of the United States – did not come true, and this was not only a matter of "democratic transition failure," that is, of the failed evolution of China and Russia into democratic systems. Something far worse happened. Over the years, a gradual "reverse" process took place among the States that were commonly considered as "democracies." Examples are before our eyes, many and growing in number: In Europe, we find Hungary, Poland, and Turkey, in South America, Brazil and Venezuela, while strong forces seem to be driving other, fully democratic, countries such as France, Italy, and Spain, in the same direction.

What is the reason for this withering of democracy in a growing number of countries? There is no single reason, but many, that vary from country to country. Three of the reasons are, as stated, general in character.

The first, perhaps more important than the others, is tied to the perception of the (one could call it) "confiscation" of the sovereignty of single nations by the actors of the global economy and of the powerful international organizations, a confiscation that – many believe – voids all contents of national politics and seems to weaken the significance of elections. This perception, right or wrong, triggers a sense of frustration toward elected representatives, accused of being unable to defend the power and interests of the people.

There is a second reason, this time tied to the use of digital media. Politics, in the digital age, has ceased to be a competition between alternative projects aimed at resolving problems not only of the present but also of the future and instead has become an activity carried out with one's eyes fixed on the day to day, ending up a mere mending of thing as they are, losing thereby any ability to see any future perspective. In other words, the continuous quest for consent asphyxiates any action by governments. Representative democracy, simply put, becomes short of breath (as sometimes happens to athletes) and struggles to obtain the results expected of it.

To these two reasons can be added a third. There are in fact growing difficulties in decision-making due to the increasing radicalization in the political systems, in which, especially on the most important and controversial issues, the parliaments are paralyzed; with the added risk that when the parliaments do come to a decision, due to one side prevailing over the other, the decision is strongly unilateral, divisive, and thus a source of conflicts and extended resistance to compliance.

Together, these three reasons entail that "politics" comes to be perceived by the general public as a "fight for seats." And too often the very same politicians interpret politics in the same way. Hence, politics becomes a fight over appointments and their ensuing benefits that the "politicians" undertake to their own advantage, neglecting the public interest. Things being as they are, every wider sectors of the population, short of great resources and whose image of the world coincides by and large with that of their home land, seek refuge within the walls of the State, of a State that preserves intact the outer semblance of democracy but not its real essence – the protection of liberties; of a State inside which these sectors find, one after the other, the reassuring figure of a plebiscitarian leader, a rushed decision-making process, a useful protective shield against a modernity that is perceived as something hostile and destructive coming from "outside," a return to the sempiternal rules defending reproduction and relations between the genders and between generations, in coherence with the handed-down meaning of hierarchy and traditional social roles.

The cost of this trend, that in the Western world has become, or could become, the majority in a troubling number of countries, consists in authoritarian practices of government. One talks, precisely, of illiberal democracy, where the system of individual and collective freedoms, the constitutional guarantees, the rule of law, the rights of political minorities appear markedly weakened. In other words, what is most particular in liberal democracy is there suffocating, agonizing.

If one combines these factors, a strong temptation arises to "skip" the (seemingly outdated) rituals of "representative" democracy in favor of a simpler plebiscitary democracy.

Notes

[1] Francis Fukuyama, *The End of History and the Last Man* (1992).
[2] Andrew Heywood, *Politics* 134 (2nd ed. 2002).
[3] John J. Mearsheimer, *The Great Delusion – Liberal Dreams and International Realities* (2018).

2 2050: A Turning Point
in the American Democracy?

To these general reasons that we have just seen, in the case of the United States, another specific reason more important than any other is ready to enter the field. The early signs of this factor are already highly visible, looming over democracy in the country. This is a decisive passage for the purpose of our discourse, and therefore, it is necessary to clarify how things stand.

The most eminent political scientists affirm, and they are certainly not mistaken, that the first and strongest defense of democracy consists in the democratic tradition of each single country, due to the fact that such tradition pertains – if and when it pertains – to the cultural heritage passed down through the generations, as is the case in France and in Anglophone countries; in other words, such defense consists in the age-old integration of democracy inside of society and of consciousness of its citizens.

In the United States, the roots of democracy are firmly embedded in that portion of the population – until today, a large majority – coming originally from the British Islands, to which are added the descendants of immigrants of the earliest period, well integrated into the predominant culture.

The demographic of this subpopulation, however, has over the years been gradually declining: 60.7% in 2017, 59.6% in 2021, and it is calculated that by about 2050, it will have dropped below 50%. Correlatively, there has been an increase in the proportion of the population consisting of, alongside Afro-Americans, men and wom-

Figure 1   Trend, verified or predicted, of the ratio among the major ethnic groups present in the United States in the period from 2015 to 2065

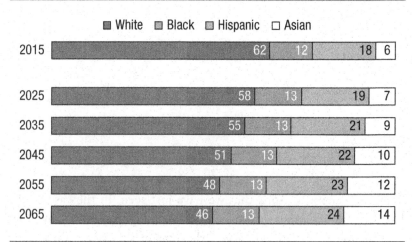

Source: D'Vera Cohn (Pew Research Center), *U.S. Demographic Trends so Far, and in the Possible Future*, available at: https://www.ncsl.org/Portals/1/Documents/Redistricting/D%27vera-Cohn.pdf.

en from Central and South America, the Middle East, and Asia. Figure 1 indicates in percentage terms the trend, verified or predicted, of the ratio among the major ethnic groups present in the United States in the period from 2015 to 2065.

Thus, as seen, in 2050 (approximately), the United States could experience a tremendous turning point, if these demographic trends are confirmed. The subpopulation, still in majority in the country, made up of those who only have one flag in their hearts and recent histories, the flag with stars and stripes, of those who repeat to themselves in all circumstances "right or wrong, my country," and who will defend to the bitter end the American creed, of those (also) who hold in their hands most of the nation's wealth and posts of influence and command; well, this subpopulation will soon be overtaken in number by the subpopulation cohabiting with it, extremely fragmented and now in a minority, in which a divided citizenship or at least less decidedly oriented one prevails.

Indeed, Afro-Americans occupy a unique position within this continually growing share of the population. There is no doubt that American culture and creed are largely shared by Afro-American people, who represent approximately 13% of the U.S. population. In many cases, from Frederick Douglass to Martin Luther King, Jr., Afro-Americans were the ones who most consistently upheld the essential values of the American Declaration of Independence, that "all men are created equal." Many of them deserve to be called "patriots" in the noblest sense of the word. However, it should be taken into account that Afro-Americans are heavily disadvantaged in terms of wealth and of leadership roles, as well as the chances for social rise, as compared to the white population. Around 2050, in a possibly chaotic situation, significantly poor standards of living might put their interests ahead of their loyalty to the existing system.

The firm adherence to democracy by the remaining share of the population, that does not identify, or not totally, with the foundations of Anglo-Protestant culture,[1] the cornerstone of the American creed, is undoubtedly less established. These are ethnic groups who have not always had the democratic culture as their own political heritage, or who have never experienced it, who have not had democracy as an existential element in their culture. In the meantime, the assimilation of the several existing cultures into the basic culture of the country faces ever greater difficulties. One factor that plays a major role in this context is the so-called new technologies. Technology, while enabling anybody to link with the whole world, also pushes everybody, at the same time, into an asocial condition. The fragmentation of collective bodies stands – inter alia – as a straightforward consequence of this scenario, running counter to the very spirit of the community and slowing down the roots in American society of these peoples, who have often recently immigrated in the country.

A second element should be added, with the same relevance as the first one. As the population made up of people of British or Irish origins, and living generations of earlier date immigrants,[2] decreases, faced with the prospect of becoming a minority in the country in the near future, frustration and rage could grow within them. These feelings gradually push ever further away any attitude of respect and tolerance toward different cultures that underpins democracy.[3] In this quota of the population, the will to preserve the values (that might be called primordial) in which they believe could arise. At the same time, they may want to preserve the political and financial privileges they enjoy and have always enjoyed. In such a context, whose early signs can already be discerned, chaos and violence are going to build up; and within all of this, individual cases of folly and political disruption may lurk hidden, ready to explode. Let us take as an example the entry into the scene of a forceful President whose behavior enables him to garner and organize the rising frustration and anger of those in that large part of the country that are willing to defend their own interests at the expense of a breakdown of democratic rule and custom. Let us imagine this President as a person with strong charismatic leadership who is not interested in keeping constitutional legality, who becomes the champion of traditional identity – within which "family values" play an increasingly central role, becoming a politicized subsystem that strongly draws together "Power" and "Religion" as a form of Christianity strongly tied to traditional values. Furthermore, let us consider that this President becomes the defender (behind the screen of those values) of the economic and controlling interests of that segment of the country.

At this point, it is also possible that democracy will short-circuit. On the one hand, it will be waived by the part of the population that are best placed to defend it, and by the President who is its representative; one the other hand, it will be defended by another portion of the population that does not have democracy in its DNA and is thus less able to respond "democratically." This situation could be defined as a (possible) "Latin-American deviation" of U.S. democracy.

Certainly, the perspective foreshadowed so far could very well be debunked, claiming it belongs to the realm of political fiction, maintaining instead that the United States is a hybrid nation, where numerous social groups live together side by side, such as the Afro-Americans, Hispanics, Asians, and Islamists, who albeit not of English or Irish origin are in any case simply Americans, just like the other members of the United States. This, one could validly affirm, is the very strength of the United States: American culture is not delimited, like that of France or Germany, but is instead a hybrid culture and has always been so. It is the strength of this great country: It is young, and will always bounce back. But it is also possible that at the acid test of 2050 or even earlier, as that date nears, and with the conflict – not so different from a civil war – that is today tearing apart the United States, demonstrates that this is not the case. A strong signal that seems to reveal a different reality lies in the fact that exponents of the Alt(ernative) Right are already preparing themselves, far in advance, to become the core Republican representatives at the Federal Congress and in other key positions at State level, following the midterm elections that will be held in November 2022. This means that ever-growing social forces are already on the move with the aim to tackle something that in the eyes of these forces constitutes a grave and imminent danger: That the subpopulation about to become the majority in the near future might overturn, in its favor, the influence lines and traditional economic and political equilibrium.

As it is easy to understand, a "low tide" phase of democracy might affect (and there is good chance) even the United States, in a not too far future.

The following reflections stem from this worrying premise. American democracy[4] is the principal defense barrier and the element of steadfastness for other democracies existing in the world. Its proper functioning bolsters them, its eventual decline would jeopardize them. It is this reason that has prompted us to write this book, albeit foreigners to the United States, to offer a contribution in defense of what is a precious asset to those who love democracy in general, and that of their own country. Thus, what we will do in this book is – to use a metaphor – to "scan" the U.S. political system to identify, starting from the constitutional issues that emerged during the Trump presidency, the weak points disclosed in that system. Consequently, we will try to make some suggestions to "stitch the tears," one by one. In this way, the U.S. system might be more ready to face turbulent times that will certainly come.

Notes

[1] On the foundations of Anglo-Protestant culture, essential elements of American identity and of the very way of conceiving and "living" democracy in that country, see Samuel P. Huntington, *Who Are We? The Challenges to American National Identity* 37–105 (2004).

[2] Also from further descents, for example, Italians, European Jews, and Arabs.

[3] Already in 1998, Robert Dahl wondered: "…as the twentieth century draws to a close, it is still unclear whether the historical practice of assimilation will be able to positively confront the growing presence in America of a Hispanic minority and other minority groups with a well-defined identity. Is the United States destined to become a multicultural society in which assimilation will no longer ensure peaceful and democratic management of cultural conflicts?". Robert Dahl, *On Democracy* 161 (1st ed. 1998).

[4] Throughout this book, the use of the adjective "American" refers only to the United States of America.

3 What Good Trump Has Left behind Him

Donald Trump was the one who, as President, interpreted first and well in advance the feeling of reaction which, although concealed, characterizes a wide part of the ethnic-cultural group that, up to now, is still dominating, but perceives that threat of a possible, significant redistribution of wealth and leadership roles within society. Donald Trump was also the one who endeavored to stabilize the existing economic and social scenario, even if this resulted in a reckless use of presidential powers and of the Constitution.

Hence, on the one hand, it would be wrong to assume – as many secretly do – that Trump only thought about Trump and went out of his way to harness the worst features of American society in an unprincipled way to achieve and retain power. On the other hand, it would be blatantly prosaic to simply depict Trump as a threat to American democracy – for instance, Richard Nixon was not far behind during the Watergate era. Ultimately, it would be too shallow to describe Trump as the most extravagant violator of some of constitutional norms. The reality is quite different. The Trump presidency was one of a kind, and different from all previous ones. It was a "warning" of what might happen in the near future, in case the process of assimilation – that, until present, worked more or less well – turns out to be insufficient. This aspect will be analyzed throughout this work.

One fact should be pointed out straight away. Donald Trump, certainly not out of any goodness of heart, did leave behind him one very valuable lesson. This lesson was left behind for everybody: For those who did not recognize the truth it contained, and for those who, albeit recognizing it, neglected or chose to ignore it. This lesson shows that in the United States, not unlike in other countries, democracy is not something destined to exist *sub specie aeternitatis* that always replicates automatically but is a perishable good that can easily shatter.

Yes, it is true, the American system includes a sophisticated safeguard mechanism, due to a vast network of agencies of various sizes and natures. Within this network, agencies check and balance each other such that none of them can, by overly abusing its power, endanger democracy itself. Power, in a nutshell, is used as the antidote to power. In addition, one should consider the "rigid" character of the Constitution, that regulates in general terms the order of precedence and competencies of the branches of government; and the judicial review, that mandates the courts of the country, and in the last instance, the federal Supreme Court, to prevent violations of the "Higher Law" from going unpunished. A third factor of defense of American democracy is the stabilizing role played by the "body" of lawyers and a strong, independent judiciary. And there are also the free press and the free spirit of the American people. All of this is true. It is also true, however, that this line of defense does not seem – under certain conditions – unbreakable, and that a well thought out strategy can trigger large cracks and irreparable erosion (Part Four).

Two questions, very different from each other, but both relevant to this point, remain unanswered. The first: Why has such a robust and firmly rooted democracy not quickly and peremptorily rejected Trump, as it should have done? Such rejection reaction only occurred following the election of Joseph (Joe) Biden and moreover only after the dramatic events of Capitol Hill, that impelled the House Speaker Nancy Pelosi on January 13, 2021 to define Trump himself "a clear and present danger to the nation."[1] The second: Does the American system have any antibodies,[2] maybe not yet charted, or engaged, to prevent and quell an authoritarian turning point that leaves intact the shell of democracy while betraying it in substance?

The aim of this work is to answer these questions.

4 Donald Trump, a Bolt from the Blue or the Harbinger of a Storm?

Donald Trump's presidency deserves an in-depth analysis in all its aspects. Only in this way, will it become clear that his has not been a presidency like many others, albeit characterized by anomalies. Rather, the Trump presidency has been the prelude to something alarming that looms on the horizon of American democracy.

Already at first blush, certain unique features stand out. The first feature consists of a blend of nationalisms: They are adjoining to some extent, but they also differ among themselves, at least in principle. Let us take a better look.

From the very first day, Trump waved the flag of conservative nationalism. This type of nationalism – summed up in Trump's slogan "America First" – comprises a set of three elements. The first is sovereignism, that on the international arena is expressed as a policy against limitations on sovereignty in favor of international entities: "Retake our sovereignty" is the most commonly used formula to denote this specific aspect. The second element is economic protectionism; and the third is "neoliberalism" in domestic economic policy, entailing an idea of continuous and unlimited economic growth, deregulation, with the State as a mere "night watchman," and competition as the only organizing principle of economic and social life.

In Trump's hands, sovereignism and economic protectionism have together threatened the unravelling of the very support structure of the world order conceived after the Second World War: Politically, breaking up the United Nations (UN), born of unwavering faith in the future and intended as to build a solidarity network among States and peoples; and, economically, risking a death blow to the principle of free trade among Nations, on which many international institutions are grounded: From the World Trade Organization (WTO) to the International Monetary Fund (IMF) to the World Bank. At the domestic level, neoliberalism spawned the disdain, that characterized the whole Donald Trump presidency, for all issues related to the protection of the environment.

This perspective explains some of the flagrant and grievous "stances" taken by President Trump and likewise some of his sensational and severe measures. In this way is explained, for example, Trump's brutal reprimand of the UN at his maiden speech delivered to General Assembly (September 25, 2017) and repeated at his second address (September 22, 2020), where he accused the UN of being a global body not interested in the needs of sovereign peoples. He asserted: "But only when you take care of your own citizen, will you find a true basis for international cooperation,"[1] thereby instigating the belief, increasingly common in our day, of a split between "power" – wielded elsewhere and aimed mainly at cheating and swindling people – and "representation," stripped of all power; and thus the ensuing idea that elections, as well as public control over representatives' political action, are worthless. This is also the origin of that "sovereignty protectionism" that has hollowed out many democracies, and threatens to empty more. In this light we must read the withdrawal of the United States, decided by President Trump, from important international organizations or multilateral treaties: From the Paris Climate Agreement; from the World Health Organization (WHO); from the United Nations Educational Scientific and Cultural Organization (UNESCO); and furthermore from the Optional Protocol annexed to the Vienna Convention on Diplomatic Relations (VCDR); from the Universal Postal Union (UPU) and the Trans-Pacific Partnership, as well as from the UN Human Rights Council. A similar logic, grounded on protectionism and "domestic neoliberalism," explains the full scale trade war used by President Trump as a weapon, in turn, of political pressure against certain countries, and of economic defense in terms of other countries; a trade war seemed to amuse Trump the way youngsters enjoy PlayStation: "When a country (USA) is losing many billions of dollars on trade with virtually every country it does business with, trade wars are good, and easy to win. Example, when we are down 100 billion of dollars with a certain country and they get cute, don't trade anymore – we win big. It's easy!"[2] And this also explains the wildcat deregulation pursued by the Trump Administration in the field of environment legislation, social welfare and labor market.

From this point of view, Trump's nationalism – notwithstanding the reckless exuberance of his political actions – is not far from the nationalism that seems to be cherished by a significant slice of the American *élites*.[3]

To conservative nationalism, comprising sovereignty and protectionism abroad and neoliberalism at home, the Trump presidency has been appending, here too from the onset, a different type of nationalism, that political sociologists define as "cultural nationalism." Apart from the formal link (that may or may not exist) with "white supremacist" wings, self-declaredly nostalgic of slavery or even explicitly Nazi-inspired, culturalism is an interpretation of the differences in mind-set and behavior characterizing various peoples that – at least in principle – stands in stark contrast to classic racism. While "old style" racism assumes that biological heredity dooms peoples to be what they are, cultural nationalism underlines the molding force and binding nature of traditions. Thus, in the name of their own cultural identity, a determined community may demand the right to non-contamination and, consequently, can insist that all those having "other" customs, values and behavior be kept at a safe distance. Which means that there is no need to cite racist doctrines in order to invoke the right to segregation and to justify policies of identity closure.[4]

From here and on these lines were determined the restrictive policies in terms of immigration, pursued by President Trump through executive orders that, as such, bypassed Congress. Examples are the project to block entry into the United States to citizens of (and coming from) Islamic countries, the so-called (Muslim) travel ban, and also the so-called border wall or U.S. Mexico barrier.

In this regard, the "people" essentially addressed by Trump – and in whose name he proclaims to speak and operate with the aim to safeguard their values and interests – are the millions of whites[5] of long-standing or more recent immigration. These are the people who, more than all others, adhere to the traditional identity values, who – having known better than others how shape their own destiny – hold a major part of political and financial resources and instruments of social control of the country. Certainly, Trump did not address the rest of the population, composed of Afro-Americans, Hispanics, Asians, and women and men from Middle Eastern countries.[6]

While conservative nationalism does not give rise to many problems in terms of threats to democracy, and provides for economic policies that are all perfectly legitimate, conversely cultural nationalism cloaks aspects that are extremely threatening for the democratic system. In a cultural nationalist view, "people" does not mean "everybody" without exceptions but is understood as a collective body. Thus, "people" comes to identify only that part of the population (and of the electorate) that approves and supports identarian policies. This gives rise to an important outcome from the perspective of democratic theory. The will of the "people" understood as "everybody" without exception in fact needs verification by means of periodical and fair electoral procedures. The will of the "people" considered as a homogeneous, collective body can instead be presumed, with no need for such "counting" procedure; and, furthermore, as there is no place for disagreement within and among the "people," the issue of rights of political minorities simply does not exist. This explains the otherwise inexplicable statement, made by Trump while the 2020 presidential election was still underway, that Biden's success was "a fraud," and victory was "stolen" from Trump himself.

In the same view, Trump attempted to undermine trust in federal courts, by promoting in public opinion the idea that the best judge is not the one who administers justice impartially but the one who interprets and applies the law according to the will and interests of the "people." This approach is in line with an identarian vision. A judge who does that is a good judge; one who does not is instead a bad judge and should be branded as such for public contempt. The same applies to journalists, and to opposition politicians.

At this point, it is possible to draw a partial conclusion based on the things we have said so far. Donald Trump, who cast himself (as written in the *New York Times* of September 6, 2020) the harbinger of possible future turbulence in American democracy, who was also in some ways the source of the second Great American Wound, the United States Capitol attack on January 6, 2021, has adopted a government strategy that has made abundant use of policies soliciting popular consensus, seeking to revive national pride (to Make America Great Again), and the American dream at the same time, by means of protectionism and tax cuts, flanked however by a less visible brake, made of "walls" and bottlenecks, on access to citizenship that means a brake on the right to vote of would-be U.S. citizens, and a cut to rights more tied to modernity: To sexual and reproductive rights, women's health and rights, the so-called "global gag rule," following a worrying tradition tracing back to the Reagan and Bush Administrations; as well as another example: LGBT rights.

Notes

[1] Stewart M. Patrick, *Donald Trump's Disjointed and Misleading UN Address,* Council on Foreign Relations (Sept. 22, 2020), https://www.cfr.org/blog/donald-trumps-disjointed-and-misleading-un-address.

[2] *Trade Wars, Trump Tariff and Protectionism Explained,* B.B.C. News (Mar. 2, 2018), https:/www.bbc.com/news/world-43512098.

[3] Brian C. Rathbun, *Does One Right Make a Realist? Conservatism, Neoconservatism, and Isolationism, the Foreign Policy Ideology of American Elites,* 123 Pol. Sci. Q. 271–299 (2008).

[4] Andrew Heywood, *Politics* 108 (2d ed. 2002); Luciano Pellicani, *Dalla società chiusa alla società aperta,* 362–363 (2001). On the use of the identity rationale to suggest adherence to the terrorist ideology as an alternative to the traditional state, see Arianna Vedaschi, *Da al-Qa\`ida all'IS: il terrorismo internazionale si è fatto Stato?,* 66 Rivista trimestrale di diritto pubblico 41 (2016).

[5] The term "white" is used here as a group of people varying over time, referred to all those who, based on different historic and cultural paths, came

to share the U.S. traditional values (especially those linked to the Republican party's ideology) and way of life.

[6] At least those ones, among these categories, who are not perceived as "included" in U.S. identity and traditions. See *supra* note 4.

5 Populism, Political Communication, and Trumpism

The jumble of separate elements, that, all together, have characterized the Trump presidency, includes two more factors to be added to the variants of nationalism as described. We are talking about "populism," more exactly right-wing "populism"; in particular, reference is to techniques (recklessly and skillfully) used by President Trump to "manipulate" public opinion.[1]

The term "populism" identifies a growing perception among public opinion: That nowadays "representative" democracy does not represent enough, or not at all, people's "real needs"; and those democratic procedures do nothing but feed a class of professional politicians who, instead of serving the country, use "representation" to serve (overtly or covertly) their own interests. Trump duly proclaimed, on the day of his inauguration, that: "...we are transferring power from Washington D.C. and giving it back to you, the people... The establishment protected itself but not the citizens of our country."

On this basis, the word "populism" took on two alternative meanings: On the one hand, it evokes "direct" democracy, the "people in government"; on the other hand, "plebiscitary" democracy. These two forms of "democracy" have in common the rejection of representative politics, its rules, and its language. "Plebiscitary" democracy, as against "direct" democracy however has two advantages. First, it provides for the presence of a governmental structure – a precondition of any mode of the exercise of power – placed in the hands of an elected/acclaimed President who is the "spokesperson" and in any case the true "interpreter" of people's real needs. Second, it enables the President to manage the political agenda and to make political compromises, both at the domestic and international level. These are two essential aspects in public policymaking. Trump's populism is – this must be specified – a right-wing "populism" that continuously taunts, almost with contempt, laws adopted on the basis of "representative" democracy, and calls, more or less openly, to disobey them in the name of a "democracy" that recognizes "other" laws and "another" order.

The other element, along with "populism," that has deeply characterized the Trump presidency has been the reckless use of political communication. His communication hinged on a key principle: A few "high impact" phrases repeated continuously, regardless of whether true or far from the truth, since falsehood can turn into truth if it becomes such in the minds of the majority of the population. This mode of political communication, whether or not inspired by Steve Bannon,[2] seemed to apply to the letter to the criteria laid down by Adolf Hitler in *Mein Kampf* for propaganda in totalitarian regimes, and that was in fact employed by Goebbels in the years of the Nazi dictatorship.

> Propaganda must not investigate the truth objectively and, in so far as it is favourable to the other side, present it according to the theoretical rules of justice; yet it must present only that aspect of the truth which is favourable to its own side. [...] The receptive powers of the masses are very restricted, and their understanding is feeble. On the other hand, they quickly forget. Such being the case, all effective propaganda must be confined to a few bare essentials and those must be expressed as far as possible in stereotyped formulas. These slogans should be persistently repeated until the very last individual has come to grasp the idea that has been put forward. [...] Every change that is made in the subject of a propagandist message must always emphasize the same conclusion. The leading slogan must of course be illustrated in many ways and from several angles, but in the end one must always return to the assertion of the same formula.[3]

This communication strategy complies with the principle, typical of the Nazi regime, whereby the more a lie is repeated the more people become convinced that the lie is the truth. Trump's last, most flagrant lie was: The result of the election was reversed; we won it! "The world knows Trump won." This lie was repeated ad infinitum, obsessively. The aim: To discredit, together with the President-elect, the majority principle, the cornerstone of representative democracy. It was from here, from this reckless communication policy, that the assault of the "true American patriots" on Capitol Hill, on January 6, 2021, would gain its momentum.

Given these general premises, it is now possible to draw a conclusion. Donald Trump was the first President, by approach and by ideology,[4] to display the ability (and the will) to catalyze positive and negative feelings and feelings triggered by the rapid demographic shift underway in the American population, and to steer the presidency and the Constitution in order to retain the traditional values as well as political and financial resources of those – the old stock white Americans – who, in the future, will become a (albeit large) minority in the country. Then, after Trump, will come others like Trump.

Notes

[1] President Donald Trump, Full Inaugural Address (Jan. 20, 2017).

[2] Bannon served as an advisor to President Trump during the first seven months of his term.

[3] Adolf Hitler, *Mein Kampf* IV (James Murphy trans., Hutchinson & Co. in association with Harst & Blackett 1939) (1925).

[4] Taking cue from some traits of Trump's political action, as well as the unscrupulous use he was making of public communication, Jason Stanley, Professor of Political Philosophy at Yale University, has come to provocatively call Donald Trump "a fascist": Jason Stanley, *How Fascism Works – The Politics of US and them*, YouTube (2020), https://www.youtube.com/watch?v=agX5v7h4_1g. It is clear that the word "Fascism" appears far away and extreme if used with reference to the United States, a country that not only has never known, not even for a day, Fascism in government, but that can also be considered, in a certain sense, the anti-fascist country *par excellence*, having, in the years from 1941 to 1945, mainly borne on its shoulders the weight of the war against Nazi-Fascism. That said, Stanley recognizes in Trump attitudes and traits that seem to coincide with those key points that Stanley himself identifies as characterizing Fascism: (a) the continuous search for an enemy to fight associated with the strong

opposition between "us" and "them," and "them" pointed out as the ene-my; (b) the cohesion of the group, "us," to be deployed against "them," the enemies; and (c) the truth overpowered by power, a power that is neither afraid nor has any qualms about drowning the truth under an avalanche of lies.

Part Two
Signs of the Breaking of Democratic Rules and Practices

6 Trump and the U.S. Constitution, One Premise and Four Events

The ideological background of the Trump Administration tells us a lot, but not the whole story. So it is worth taking a step forward and then proceeding to examine four events having constitutional relevance. These, more and better than others, can show Trump's reckless flippancy in approaching and handling the Constitution. The first instance regards the attempt, made by Trump and the staff of legal experts who assisted him, to claim that the false or reluctant witness given by the President and/or others in support of the President before an independent authority was no more than a legitimate type of self-defense in the face of "unfair" accusations moved against the President by political adversaries.

Other two more policies relating to them followed, to which the Trump Administration devoted much of its initial energies. One is the policy introduced under the proclaimed need to prevent the infiltration of Muslim terrorists in the national territory. The other is the intensely aggressive policy to combat illegal immigration, in particular immigration coming from "porous" border between the United States and Mexico, a border that was even displayed to the public opinion as the doorway for an uninterrupted flow of criminal manpower. These two policies seem to share the same ideological basis: That of unrestrainedly defending, by exalting them, the more traditional values of the most blatantly "American" society against any possible "contamination" coming from "other" cultures. The path of these policies, both politically and legally, was a very rough one. More detail will be given further on.

The fourth instance regards Trump's ambivalent attitude before and during the "patriots" attack on Capitol Hill.

Considered together, all these instances derive – directly or indirectly – from a common premise, that is, the "vision" that Trump has of the American presidency. So, we should start from this "vision" and keep the analysis of the events for the paragraphs that immediately follow.

7 A Premise. The Presidency According to Trump

In order to understand, from a constitutional point of view, the President's attempt to weaken (if not dismantle) the rules and procedures of the American representative democracy, a premise should be made. There is an idea (theorized by some but unknown in practical terms) of the presidential role and of the powers consequently annexed to such role, from which that President saw fit to draw inspiration for his government actions. The idea can be summarized as the "imperial executive" theory, a radical version of the unitary executive theory.

To understand better, one just needs to read the transcript from the Senate hearing of January 16, 2019, of Neil J. Kinkopf, Professor of Law at the Georgia State University.[1] In providing an argument for his opinion against the nomination – which then took place – of William P. Barr as Attorney General[2] of the United States,[3] Professor Kinkopf outlines as follows the two concepts of unitary executive theory and imperial executive theory, as well as the shift from the first concept (in itself already problematic) to the second:

> The imperial executive theory is an extreme view of the so-called unitary executive theory of presidential power. At its core, that theory regards as unconstitutional any law that limits the President's authority to supervise the work of officers and other subordinates in the executive branch. The main concern is to maintain a clear, unfettered chain of command within the Administration. Where the unitary executive theory is aimed at preserving the President's

ability to supervise subordinates, Barr's recently elaborated theory holds that statutes may not limit or regulate the ways in which the President exercises his executive power. Under this theory of "imperial" presidential power, the President is free to exercise his vast constitutional authority as he sees fit during his term. The only checks on his exercise of executive power are (the extremely limited) Congress's power to hold oversight hearings, impeach the President, and make political considerations. Under this vision, the President and the Administration may exercise their executive power free from any legal constraint.

To this regard, Professor Kinkopf had no doubts: "What remains is an executive power of breath-taking scope, subject to negligible limits. This is not the presidency our founders contemplated; this is not the presidency our Constitution meant to embody. This vision of presidential power is contrary to the constitutional system of checks and balance that lies at heart of our Constitution." Hence, the conclusion that Neil Kinkopf reaches: "William Barr's view of the Constitution exalts presidential power, ignores Congress's legitimate legislative power, and minimizes the role of judiciary."

Neil Kinkopf does not say so explicitly, but it is a fact that the imperial executive theory, credited by Bill Bar, was indeed the (clumsy) attempt to redeem all the main violations of the rule of law perpetrated by Donald Trump during his four-year mandate, by laying across them a veil of legal respectability; Barr's attempt being one that Neil Kinkopf showed to be totally unfounded.

Notes

[1] *Nomination of the Honorable William Pelham Barr to be Attorney General of the United States: Hearing on Attorney General Nomination before the S. Comm. on the Judiciary* (2019), https://www.judiciary.senate.gov/meetings/01/16/2019/nomination-of-the-honorable-william-pelham-barr-to-be-attorney-general-of-the-united-states.

[2] The Attorney General is the head of the Department of Justice and at the same time is the main legal advisor to the President.

[3] *Nomination of William P. Barr to Be Attorney General of the United States before the Committee on the Judiciary* (2019) (Statement of Neil J. Kinkopf).

8   Trump, the Mueller Report and Obstruction of Justice

In the report written by the Special Counsel,[1] Robert Mueller, at the end of the inquiry on the so-called Russiagate (March 22–April 18, 2019), there are two conclusions, which appear to be (but actually are not) parallel and unrelated to each other. The first conclusion supplies an answer to the fundamental question behind the creation (on March 17, 2017) of the Special Counsel on the investigation into Russian interference in the 2016 presidential election by the Deputy Attorney General, Rod Rosenstein. Mueller's conclusion in his report is that Trump was presumably not involved in the interference of the Russian government in the presidential elections of 2016; an interference that (as was its purpose) damaged Hillary Clinton, the democrat candidate, and favored Donald Trump. The second conclusion drawn in Special Counsel Mueller's report is that, during the inquiry, there were a certain number of episodes that constitute obstruction of justice and were perpetrated by Donald Trump himself, through an illegal – due to conflict of interests – exercise of his powers. More precisely: Special Counsel Mueller only describes those episodes, without drawing any conclusion from them, and this on the basis of the unassailable argument that the Constitution reserves scrutiny of the most serious of crimes which the President of the House of Representatives might be accused of to the impeachment procedure.

The validity of the second conclusion as a basis to justify an impeachment proceeding against Trump was contested by his lawyer

Rudolph Giuliani: If the main crime did not exist, claimed Giuliani, then the obstruction of justice cannot be considered as a crime. The logic of the argument, in other words, is that the obstruction of justice is none other than legitimate self-defense against an unfair trial.

This argument, which we will talk about in a moment, evidently aims at hiding a crucial matter of fact. The obstruction of justice, committed by Trump and that Rudolph Giuliani in no way denies, and in fact admits by "justifying" it, has touched upon one of the most sensitive spots of democratic institutions – the transparency and honesty of the electoral process, and in particular the one relative to the election of the person who, in the position of Chief Executive, is to become the epicenter of the system of government – as well as some basic principles of the Constitution.

One of these principles is the independence which the President must always and by all means be granted in managing his role and in exercising the powers that the Constitution assigns him, this independence being protected by Article II, Section I, cl. 7, Constitution which prohibits any kind of influence in presidential decisions coming from federal or state subjects, and most of all, any influence coming from foreign powers that could be in the position to blackmail, interfere or influence those decisions.

A second principle affected by obstruction of justice is the obligation of the President, implicit in a series of rules such as the one stated by Article II, Section I, cl. 5, Constitution, of exercising the powers assigned to him in the exclusive interest of the United States, without having to be subject to, or agreeing to be subject to any foreign interference. We are, in other words, at a crossroad. Can a President defend democracy and the Constitution and work to the exclusive service of the country; or can he, in actual fact, accept, by tearing apart the Constitution, that a foreign country may condition to its own advantage national politics. One thing the President cannot do is to follow both courses.

Let us now return briefly to the argument according to which the obstruction of justice that took place in the course of the Mueller investigation is nothing more than an instrument of self-defense. This is truly a phantasmagorical argument. The inquiry that was carried out, albeit among pressures and a myriad attempts of stopping it,[2] by special Counsel Robert Mueller's staff, had the purpose – as perusal in such cases – of ascertaining the truth of the matter via an independent procedure. So it is either one or the other: Either Trump was actually unaware of the facts that actually did play in his favor, but without having any active role in them, and therefore having all the interest in loyally and fully collaborating with the Special Counsel Mueller in order for his complete deniability to be confirmed beyond any reasonable doubt – and indeed self-defense exercised by someone innocent against the verification of his innocence is a blatant contradiction; or Trump is not at all uninvolved in the facts, and therefore the obstruction of justice is nothing more than laborious attempt to duck his responsibilities.

In any case, the American people had, and still have, the right to know, on the basis of a "fair and not obstructed" procedure, whether Donald Trump did or did not usurp his presidential role and powers thanks to a "rigged" election; and therefore if his oath of loyalty to the Constitution, made in the hands of John Roberts, Chief Justice of the Supreme Court of United States, was, or was not, perjury.

At this point, it is clear that the mutual non-interference of the two conclusions that substantiate the Mueller report leaves us in wide margins of doubt. The question to which only Congress will have to give an answer is whether the obstruction of justice committed by Trump in the course of the inquiry carried out by Robert Mueller did or not prevent ascertaining if Trump "cheated" in the challenge for the presidential elections of 2016. But the fact the Mueller Report may be the premise and the starting point for a process of impeachment against Donald Trump may help explain a circumstance that would otherwise have no easy explanation. Once having received, on March 22, 2019, the Report, having read and summarized it – we do not know how accurately – in four meagre little pages, and then having duly metabolized them, Attorney General William Barr – who was chosen by Trump – instituted, starting from October 19, 2020, a new Special Counsel, appointing John Durham, District of Connecticut Attorney, for the role and whose functions practically took up those of Robert Mueller.[3]

Notes

[1] On the institution of the so-called special investigations, also from a comparative point of view, see Luigi Melica, *Special Investigations e comparabilità, dagli U.S.A. all'America Latina* (2021).

[2] Andrew Weissmann, *Where Law Ends: Inside The Mueller Investigation* (2020). See also *id.*, *Where Law Ends: Inside the Mueller Investigation*, YouTube (2020), https://www.youtube.com/watch?v=beaUVJYO1a0.

[3] Josh Blackman, *The Statutory Authority for Barr's Appointment of Durham as Special Counsel*, Lawfare (Dec. 2, 2020), https://www.lawfareblog.com/statutory-authority-barrs-appointment-durham-special-counsel. If the Russiagate has been gradually fading away, to then definitively disappear from the political radar, this is due, at least in part, to the so-called Ukraine affair. According to the Intelligence Committee of the House of Representatives, it was a new attempt to hijack the presidential elections, this time organized and carried out personally by Donald Trump in order to get rid of his rival Joe Biden in the race for the White House and thus obtain the certainty of re-election as President in 2020. In more than 300 pages of the conclusive report, the Intelligence Committee accuses Trump of having abused his powers and exerted very strong pressure on the Ukrainian government in order to provide or fabricate evidence of wrongdoing by Joe Biden's son, Hunter, who had worked in Ukraine for some time. Donald Trump allegedly threatened the Ukrainian government with blocking the supply of weapons and other strategic material to that country. On December 18, 2019, the House of Representatives, based on the findings of the inquiry conducted by the Intelligence Committee for about seven months, formulated the formal indictment in the impeachment proceedings opened against Trump for "abuse of power" and "obstruction of Congress." The Senate, to which the Constitution assigns the task of making the judgment, acquitted him of these charges on February 5, 2020. All Republicans, except one, voted for acquittal; all Democrats – a minority in the Senate at that time – voted for the removal of Trump from office. It should be added that even before Trump's impeachment by the House of Representatives, no less than 500 law professors from the most prestigious American universities, including Yale, Harvard, and Berkley, wrote an open letter addressed to the two branches of Congress stating that there was "overwhelming evidence" that Trump had pressured "a foreign government" in order to "pervert" the presidential election that was now just around the corner. See also Katy Grimes, *UC Berkeley History Professor's Open Letter against BLM, Police Brutality and Cultural Orthodoxy,* California Globe (June 14, 2020).

9   The So-Called (Muslim) Travel Ban Tested against the First Amendment

Trump's policy was characterized by the will to preserve, and perhaps restore in their purity, the most traditional values of "white" American society against the danger of spreading in the country values and lifestyles coming from a world seen as alien and potentially destructive. This will, albeit hidden behind the claimed intent to protect the United States against the incumbent threat of Islamic terrorism, took shape through three consecutive executive orders, different from one another but with a very similar rationale.

The Clash over the First Version of the Travel Ban

At the end of January 2017, in the early days of his office, Donald Trump, in keeping with the promises made in his electoral campaign,[1] adopted Executive Order No. 13769[2] that went by the name: "Protecting the Nation from Foreign Terrorist Entry into the United States." Based on alleged reasons of national security, the so-called travel ban 1.0 banned any citizen of seven countries,[3] all of which of Muslim majority, from entering the United States for a period of 90 days. In fact, in its first version, the ban seemed to even include legal permanent residents.[4] Simultaneously, the same order would suspend for 120 days the Refugee Admission Program,[5] regardless of the applicants' country of origin. The Secretary of State and the Secretary of Homeland Security still had the option of considering exceptions in the national interest,[6] both for requests made by foreigners coming from the banned countries and for refugees. In the case of refugees, a priority position was granted to members of religious minorities (Christian), whereas for Syrian refugees, the entry ban was extended indeterminately.

Given the immediate implementation of the presidential order and due to the White House's and the Department of Homeland Security's failure to coordinate on what procedures to follow for the execution of the order, total chaos broke out in many airports, echoed by criticism from the press and from eminent legal experts.

While chaos raged in the airports, in the competent courts, the governors of several States[7] filed motions for preliminary injunctions to Executive Order No. 13769. These motions where then joined and decided upon by the United States District Court for the Western District of Washington.

The plaintiffs reported many violations, specifically of the First Amendment and more in particular of the Establishment Clause, which ensures, among other things, equal treatment of all religions.[8] The Establishment Clause was violated by the ban because, by limiting the entry of Muslim foreigners in the U.S., it granted an evident priority to non-American Christians, which entailed the Federation's undue interference with religious matters, rather than a neutral stand before all religions.

State governors also denounced the failure to comply with the Due Process Clause, established by the Fifth Amendment, which provides that anyone involved is always offered a means of appeal against a ban on entry into U.S. territory. Much on the contrary, by not ensuring necessary guarantees of the due process, the travel ban had a significant bearing on freedom of movement, with the restriction being *sine die* in the case of Syrian refugees. Furthermore, the violation of the Fifth Amendment was denounced in relation to the Equal Protection Clause,[9] given how the ban set by the presidential provision was affecting the citizens of some countries (those of Muslim majority) differently from other foreigners, with no reasonable motivation.

One last allegation made by the governors concerned the fact that by forcing the States to apply the ban, and thereby enforcing an entry restriction based on one's country of origin, the President, that is, the federal power, was imposing (at least indirectly) the suspension of State legislation (for example, in matters of employment, housing, trade within the State), which rule out discrimination based on nationality and religious belief; hence the violation of the Tenth Amendment (delegated powers doctrine).

Additionally, by referring to the ordinary legislation rather than the Constitution, the plaintiffs denounced the Executive Order's violation of the procedures required by the Immigration and Nationality Act (INA)[10] for the release of visas. The INA forbids any form of discrimination based on race, nationality, place of birth or residency. More to the point, to deny, a priori, the possibility to make a request for refugee status would be in contrast – according to the appealers – also with other provisions of the INA,[11] that instead allow immigrants to submit to the competent authorities a request for asylum, and if applicable for refugee status. The competent authorities are then required to verify, case-by-case, whether the conditions stand up to examination for the acceptance of the request.

Last but not least, by denying refugee status to people who are at risk of torture or other inhuman and degrading treatment, the travel ban could potentially violate the United Nations Convention against Torture implemented in the U.S. legal system by the Foreign Affairs and Restructuring Act.[12]

Before examining the claims made by the plaintiffs, the District Court[13] considered the motion for preliminary injunction and granted it. In granting the injunction, the Court acknowledged, on the one hand, the risk of a permanent damage deriving from the coming into effect of the Executive Order[14] and, on the other, the strong probability that the appeal would be successful.[15] In other words, the strength of the arguments that had been put forth, from which derived, at least prognostically, the concrete chances of success of the motions made by the appealers, combined with the need to avoid irreparable harm,[16] persuaded the Court to order the suspension of the ban within the federal territory.

Challenged by this decision, President Trump openly and publicly accused the Court – which he defined, with his customary polemic and irreverent tone, a "pseudo judge" – of jeopardizing national security.[17]And, not fully content with his Twitter tirades, Trump challenged before the Court of Appeals for the Ninth Circuit[18] the decision taken by the District Court. More specifically, referring to the plenary powers doctrine[19] and, consequently claiming the "unreviewability" of executive orders in matters of immigration, the Trump Administration requested the immediate suspension of the temporary restraining order, adopted, as mentioned above, by Washington's District Court.

Trump's motion was nonetheless forcefully rejected per curiam by the Court of Appeals.[20] The second instance judge, agreeing with the judge of first instance on the strong chances of success of the appeals presented by the governors of the States, stated that the unreviewability thesis, confidently put forth by the Trump Administration, did in actual fact "[run] contrary to the fundamental structure of our constitutional democracy." The President, even if free to determine the purpose of his actions, meets an insuperable containment in the principle of the separation of powers, set by the Constitution. In the reasoning of the judge of appeals, if the unreviewability thesis was to prevail, the courts would be forced to silence, which not only would violate Article 3 of the Constitution but would also allow the President to bend the "Higher Law" to his own purposes, bypassing the checks and balances process.

In the meantime, the Trump Administration decided to file a motion for the suspension of the procedure, claiming the order (travel ban 1.0) would be revoked and replaced with a second version. Trump's motion was filed in the heavy fire of the press and in order to respond to the criticism of numerous legal experts.[21]

... and over the Second Version

At the beginning of March 2017, President Trump adopted Executive Order No. 13780, "Protecting the Nation from Foreign Terrorist Entry into the United States."[22] The so-called travel ban 2.0, with the purpose of providing at least statistically objective elements about the social danger posed by immigrants coming from specific areas of the globe, referred to the data of a 2017 report on terrorism delivered by the U.S. Department of State.

This second version, besides the effort to use these recognized statistical elements, appears, in its substance, very similar to the first version. However, the two versions differ, first of all, because the second explicitly excluded the use of the ban on legal permanent residents and those already holding a valid visa to enter the United Sates.[23] Travel ban 2.0 also established the suspension of the Refugee Program for 120 days, at the end of which the competent authorities would have had to decide – on case-by-case criterion – whether to grant refugee status or not. Iraq[24] was no longer in the list of banned countries. Furthermore, the ban on accepting Syrian refugees[25] was no longer permanent, and also the preference for Christian refugees was no longer a feature.

Even this second version of the ban was challenged under several aspects before the competent courts. In particular by requesting a pronouncement of constitutional illegitimacy, subject to suspension of the presidential order, the governor of the State of Hawaii denounced the following violations: Of the Establishment Clause of the First Amendment; of the Equal Protection and of the Due Process Clause, both provided by the Fifth Amendment; as well as of the prohibition of discrimination enshrined in the INA.

In mid-March 2017, the District Court of Hawaii[26] saw good chances for the success of the appeal, given the absence, in the opinion of the Court, of a sufficiently substantiated connection between the entrance in U.S. territory of migrants and refugees from the countries listed in the ban and threats to national security, as instead stated by the Trump Administration. On the contrary, according to the Court, the alleged necessity for national security had the purpose of hiding the discrimination intent toward foreigners of Muslim religion.

Two months later, in mid-May, based on the same reasons given by the District Court of Hawaii, the decision was confirmed, in second instance, by the Court of Appeals for the Ninth Circuit.[27]

Simultaneously to *Trump v. Hawaii*, the *International Refugee Assistance Project v. Trump* litigation was beginning in Maryland.

Also in this case, the Court of first instance granted the request for a preliminary injunction and suspended the order.[28] And just as in the previous case, the Court of Appeals confirmed the suspension.[29] Specifically, recalling the claims made by Trump during his electoral campaign, the Court of second instance found in the examined order an evident "anti-Muslim purpose" and therefore the requirements of the so-called Lemon test were not met.[30]

In June 2017, both the decisions of appeal, having the suspension orders been confirmed by the Courts of Hawaii and Maryland, were challenged by the Trump Administration before the Supreme Court of the United Sates. The Supreme Court,[31] as a precautionary measure, and as a partial reform of the decisions taken by the lower courts, ruled that, while waiting for a decision to be taken on the issue, the ban was to be applied to "foreign nationals who lack any *bona fide* relationship with a person or entity in the United States." In other words, the Court held that, pending on the decision, only those who could prove a "*bona fide* relationship with a person or entity in the United States" would be allowed to enter the national territory.

The looming "natural" expiry of the travel ban 2.0[32] prevented the Supreme Court from ruling on the substance of the provision.

... and over the Third Version

On September 24, 2017, the same day as the "natural expiry" of the second version of the ban, President Trump adopted Presidential Proclamation No. 9645.[33] The so-called travel ban 3.0 would, on the one hand, reconsider the list of countries affected by the measure (Chad,[34] Iran, Libya, North Korea, Somalia, Syria, Venezuela, and Yemen), also including two countries that have not a Muslim majority (North Korea and Venezuela); on the other hand, it adjusted the levels of restriction of entry to the United States in relation to the security checks made during expatriation.[35] It should also be mentioned that differently than in the previous versions, characterized by a specific expiry date, travel ban 3.0 was to be permanent.

The same plaintiffs who filed the appeal against travel ban 2.0, in October 2017, challenged this version too before the competent district Court,[36] which, as other courts with regard to previous versions of the ban, granted a suspension.[37] On this occasion, as well as finding a discriminatory effect on the sensitive area of freedom of religion, and consequently, the violation of the Establishment Clause, the Court also found that President Trump "exceeded the scope of authority." More specifically, President Trump would have exceeded the limits set by Congress in the INA, which does grant to the executive the government's policies on immigration, but still subject to the prohibition of discrimination.[38]

Similarly, as on previous occasions, the Trump Administration filed a request for suspension against the district Court's decision. In December 2017, as a precautionary measure, the Court of Appeals of the Ninth Circuit took a similar decision as the Supreme Court. More specifically, also according to the judge of second instance, the ban should continue to apply to those who could not prove to have "a *bona fide* relationship with a person or entity in the United States,"[39] and should instead be suspended for those who could satisfy the burden of proof.

While waiting for the Court of Appeals to make a pronouncement on the issue, Donald Trump hastened once again to turn to the Supreme Court.[40] The purpose of the parties involved was to verify the President's authority of limiting the entry of foreigners in the country. The Court was therefore called to evaluate travel ban 3.0 against two parameters: The first being the Establishment Clause, which grants the equal treatment of religions; the second being the Immigration National Act, against which it was to be decided whether the President was exceeding or not the powers that the Congress gave him in matters of immigration.

On June 26, 2018, the Supreme Court issued a controversial judgement, voted by a very narrow majority.[41] Once again, as we shall see very soon, the rift that divides the Court has to do with the powers that should be granted to the President in matters of national security.

The majority opinion, drafted by Chief Justice Roberts and joined by judges Alito, Gorsuch, Kennedy, and Thomas, oozes deference toward the President's prerogatives. First of all, the majority of the Court points out that, despite the prohibition of discrimination "because of the person's race, sex, nationality, place of birth, or place of residence," the law (i.e., the INA) grants the President full authority in preventing the entry of foreign citizens in federal territory, in case their presence is "detrimental to the interest of the United States." Here we would like to draw the attention on two aspects. First, that the assessment of the cause-effect relation between the presence of a foreigner in U.S. territory and the actual danger for the national interest is, according to the Court, exclusive competence of the President. The second aspect worth noting is that, still according to the Court, the President is not even required to motivate his choice or to prove this link, that is, the existence of specific reasons that may induce to recognize a threat to public security deriving from the entry in the country of a foreign citizen. Therefore, the Court – because of its jurisdictional and not political character – holds that it cannot carry out any type of verification regarding the actual existence of this causal link.

Furthermore, in the opinion of the majority, the prohibition of discrimination, established by the INA as a limit to presidential authority, should not be given extensive reading, that is, a reading that could limit President Trump's wide discretion in banning the entrance of foreigners in the States. On the contrary, according to the majority of the judges, such a limit should be understood restrictively and should apply only with regard to the release of visas, and not to the preceding and equally delicate phase of identifying the categories of foreigners entitled to make requests for visas.

Therefore, Trump did not exceed his power, given that the legislation itself (or rather the Congress) grants the President wide (if not, at least according to the majority of the Court, unlimited) discretion for selecting "categories" of foreigners entitled to request a visa.

The majority opinion then returned on the issue of discrimination when the Court proceeded to examine if there was or not a violation of the Establishment Clause of the First Amendment, which, as already mentioned, prohibits the unequal treatment of religions.

In the assessment of the compatibility of travel ban 3.0 with the Establishment Clause, the Court applied the rational basis test, that is the least "demanding" standard in assessing the constitutionality of a piece of legislation. The judges who endorsed the majority's opinion resorted to this rather pliant test based on the belief that the issue of immigration and the relative assessments of national security both require a widely deferential approach toward the political decision maker; so deferential as to render completely uninfluential in the decision the clearly discriminatory and disparaging claims made by Trump on several occasions toward those who follow Muslim beliefs.

Technically, it was sufficient for the judges to emphasize that the ban seemed clearly aimed at accomplishing a plausible and "legitimate interest" as that of controlling migration processes because of reasons of security and that, prima facie, the ban contained in the presidential order seemed in fact suitable to meet this national interest.[42]

This noticeable deference that clearly transpires from the whole argumentation of the Court, pushed Justice Kennedy, also part of the majority, to clarify (unsolicited excuse…) that at any rate, the deferential approach adopted by the Supreme Court in cases of high political significance – as undoubtedly was the one in question – certainly could not leave government officials "free to disregard the Constitution and the rights it proclaims and protects."[43]

The concern that national security may systematically become the excuse for hiding "inconvenient claims" is evident instead from the whole dissenting opinion expressed by Justice Sotomayor, which Justice Ginsburg joined.[44] Though not putting forward considerations of a psychological kind with regard to what intentions the President had, Justice Sotomayor, in reconstructing the historical background of the executive order, did not fail to observe an undoubtable "anti-Muslim animus" in Donald Trump.[45] To this regard, it is worth recalling the expression Sotomayor used: "A reasonable observer would conclude that the Proclamation was motivated by anti-Muslim animus."

What's more, Sotomayor describes the discipline that was being examined as a "religious gerrymandering"[46] and did not hesitate to compare the majority opinion to the one in *Korematsu v. the United States*.[47] Given the circumstances – according to Justice Sotomayor – the Court should not have applied the rational basis test in order to evaluate the violation of the First Amendment and, specifically, of the Establishment Clause, and should have instead at least resorted to intermediate scrutiny,[48] if not even strict scrutiny,[49] given that the safeguard of the cardinal principle of religious neutrality was at stake. In any case, even by applying the rational basis test, the conclusion should be drawn, still in the opinion of Justice Sotomayor, that even this very deferential test, would not have allowed to avoid the declaration of illegitimacy of travel ban 3.0.[50]

The strong distance between the literal tone of the provision and its actual application was then highlighted, with supporting evidence, by Justices Breyer and Kagan.[51] The two, in arguing their dissenting opinion, remarked on the fact that the concrete application of the ban appeared to be strongly biased to the disadvantage or foreigners who are Muslim, and by this argument, they proved the violation to First Amendment.[52]

Despite the authoritative dissenting opinions, the majority opinion allowed Proclamation No. 9645 to remain in effect as it had been modified by Proclamation No. 9723 of April 10, 2018.[53] Indeed, on January 31, 2020, President Trump signed Proclamation No. 9723, which set further limitations, and for an undetermined amount of time, to the entrance of immigrants coming from Eritrea, Kyrgyzstan, Myanmar, Nigeria, Sudan, and Tanzania.

As is known, travel ban 3.0 and all provisions related to it, specifically Proclamation No. 9645, Proclamation No. 9723, and finally Proclamation No. 9983 were all revoked by President Biden.[54] On January 20, 2021, the first day of his mandate, the newly elected President signed Proclamation No. 10141, with which even Executive Order No. 13780 (i.e., travel ban 2.0) was revoked. As a matter of fact, although it had been made no longer effective or applicable, in truth it still existed in the American legal system, and therefore, it was potentially applicable in the future, in case the President on duty should choose for its "revival."

A Final Remark

There are a number of considerations to highlight at this point. First of all, the fact that President Joseph Biden, as he had committed to, promptly revoked the travel ban, though showing a radical change in direction and allowing an immediate move forward, still offers no reassurance for the mid- to long term. There is no guarantee in fact that in the near or distant future, another President who thinks and acts like Trump, if not Trump himself, may not advance the same measures again. Indeed, the legitimacy of presidential operating, officialized by the Supreme Court's pronouncement in *Trump v. Hawaii*, has in actual (or better, in legal) terms, "normalized" Trump's controversial policy in matters of immigration.[55]And this is the issue to be solved or at least faced in order to avoid in the future that an "inconvenient" precedent could be used so as to corroborate similar measures.

It is therefore important to take apart, one piece at a time, the *Trump v. Hawaii* decision. This paragraph contains our contribution to this purpose.

We have seen how the objections to the travel ban focused on the issue of religious animus, according to which behind the reasons of security (the legitimate interest to protect), officially put forward by the Trump Administration, there was instead the will to deny entrance in the country to those who follow religious and social traditions that are unknown to, as well as distant from, those of the average white American. More frankly, this is a Muslim ban rather that a ban dictated by reasons of security (security-based ban), hence the alleged violation of the Establishment Clause.

Backed by this argument, the State of Hawaii and other subjects that started the litigation, demanded to call the Supreme Court to "question the intentions" and to scrutinize Trump's and his closest collaborator's animus, to probe their mind, albeit on the base of objective evidence; almost as if the Supreme Court was made of luminaries of psychology (the judgement mentions "Associate Firm of Psychology"), rather than judges. And in fact on this point, the Court was divided. Anti-Muslim animus was excluded not only by the Justices who underwrote the majority opinion but also the dissenting Justices Breyer and Kagan. The two, at least in specific reference to the literal meaning of the order examined by the Court, found no form of religious discrimination, because they did nothing more than consider what was written and refused to question the intentions (which however would have appeared clear in the application[56]). Indeed, even Justice Sotomayor, while holding[57] with conviction the argument of religious animus, considering it proven by the declarations and the behaviors of Donald Trump, both during the electoral campaign, as a candidate, and during his mandate, as President, prefaced – in her dissenting opinion – that it does not rest with the Court to explore the drafters' intentions under a psychological lens.[58]

The argument on which to focus should have perhaps been different: The Supreme Court – as all courts with powers of judicial review of political action – should have been asked to carry out an assessment of reasonableness. And especially in consideration of the issue and its delicate context, as well as the particular historical context, that is, the odd presidency in charge, the required standard should not have been substantially based on the political question doctrine. On the contrary, since reasonableness has to meet two conditions, of purpose and means, the Court should have been encouraged to verify whether the means adopted, that is an executive order aimed at preventing hundreds of thousands of foreign citizens from entering the country, was reasonable in view of the purpose of the provision under review (in this case, the need to protect national security). This evaluation could have been carried out without focusing on the religious beliefs of those foreign citizens. One should bear in mind, in fact, that the argument of religious animus did become difficult to maintain before the Court, after the timely adjustments made by the Trump Administration to the list, which already in the second version of the ban were not all Muslim majority countries.[59]

In other words, instead of questioning the purpose underlying the *ratio decidendi*, the Court should have been asked to verify the relation between the intended purpose and the adopted means, so as to show the irrationality of the provisions in question. To put it more clearly, the correct question to place before the Court should have been whether the link between the purpose and the means suggested by the provision was or was not reasonable – or "proportionate," as one would say in a European perspective. With the problem placed in this scope, the Court should have pondered whether other, less drastic, measures were available in order to safeguard security; measures that would be less damaging to the dignity of individuals and more respectful of equality of treatment.

By framing the issue in these terms, it would have maybe been possible to show in all evidence the disproportion between the means adopted and the (legitimate) ends pursued, focusing the evaluation on the means (i.e., its interdiction measure) so as to avoid questioning the intentions of the purpose (i.e., security).

Also perplexing is the insistence of the majority on the fact that other Presidents before Trump had used their power with great discretion in matters of immigration, especially when aimed at the stated intent (or better, warped by reasons) of security. Indeed, even the Trump Administration, in confronting the outraged reactions of the liberal press, did not fail to point out[60] that the measures adopted where not so different from those taken during Obama's presidency. Obama's spokesperson did however clarify that the scope of the provisions made in 2011[61] was different and directed at some Iraqi refugees who were involved in the bombing of American troops, and not applied to entire populations, with no plausible reason, as those in question.[62]

So instead of wholeheartedly claiming the continuity with the past, almost as if to ground (if not consolidate) for the future that same decision, the Court could have addressed the problem of the reasonability of the ban, applied as it was to the whole population of several countries. Following this line of reasoning, the Court could have (nay, should have) come to decide for the irrationality of the provision adopted by the Executive, in essence based on the assumed dangerousness of entire populations of individual subjects.

From this perspective, even the argument at the basis of the dissenting opinion of Justices Breyer and Kagan does not seem persuasive. In the opinion of the two Justices, the provision that places a generalized ban on the entrance in the country should be considered legitimate in the written text, because it allows some possible exceptions; but in truth, the provision is illegitimate – according to Justices Breyer and Kagan – given that these exceptions seem in practical terms almost inapplicable and consequently inexistent. It perhaps would have been more correct to turn the reasoning upside down: Regardless of the exceptions contained, the provision was to be considered illegitimate because a generalized ban on entry in the country is a disproportionate means if compared to the purpose for which it is adopted; and the exceptions, even if they were many or several, instead of few and inapplicable, were a totally uninfluential element in its judgement.

Furthermore, we believe the Court could have perhaps seized the opportunity, handed to it on a plate by the reckless behavior of the Trump presidency, to revise its traditional self-restraint in matters of security, precisely by using the delicate aspect of his migration policy. On the contrary, in the case we are analyzing, this policy, rather than unhinging it, seems to be subject to the unstoppable force of attraction of securitarian logic, now consolidated and heavily emphasized in the post 9/11 era.[63]

The case brought before the Court should have instead allowed for a prudential re-balancing of powers and a consequent rearrangement of the form of government, which over the last 20 years has become increasingly subject to the prerogatives of the Executive, also because the Supreme Court has practically abdicated when it comes to sensitive issues such as security and, more recently, migration policies. In certain historical moments, appropriate deference, though wide, toward the President's choices (even with Presidents not as unusual as Trump) does not mean granting them unlimited discretion on the delicate aspect of human rights. On the contrary, setting limits to political action, containing it from the outside, is to mark the sacred boundary between discretion and whim: The former being allowable, at times even desirable, the latter never being tolerable and certainly not in democratic governments. Setting those limits means holding in place the key principles of democracy.[64]

Donald Trump's bizarre presidency should have pushed the Supreme Court to recalibrate the check and balances system, which lies at the heart of the American political system. Instead, the Court, confronted with the vague argument of national security brought up by the Trump Administration, settled for the usual "act of faith," making matters worse by failing to scrutinize the provisions at the level of reasonability. In turn, this meant surrendering to the President the governance of migration policies, abdicating the possible and due assessment of the causal link between objectives and means and of the reasonability of the measures that were taken. This necessary assessment was indeed not carried out in the case examined, which involved the entire population of several countries. The abdication of the Court entailed that the full discretion of the President became his arbitrary behavior in the insidious terrain of choices that significantly impact on individuals' rights and freedoms. This has entailed a significant (and worrying) involution of the American democratic system.

Notes

[1] The ban had been a key issue of the campaign conducted between 2015 and 2016 by then-presidential candidate Donald J. Trump. Moreover, his official website stated that, if elected, he would order "a total and complete shutdown of Muslims entering the United States." The statement, originally posted on December 7, 2015, was later removed from the web, by the site's own managers, after strong media and political controversy ensued.

[2] Exec. Order No. 13769, 82 Fed. Reg. 8977 (Jan. 27, 2017). The measure is based on Section 212(f) of the Immigration and Nationality Act (INA), which authorizes the President to "suspend the entry of all aliens or any class of aliens" whose entry in the United States "would be detrimental to the interests of the United States."

[3] Iran, Iraq, Libya, Somalia, Sudan, Syria, and Yemen.

[4] Not explicitly excluded from the scope of the measure. Subsequently, an authoritative guidance of the White House clarifies, however, that the ban does not apply to those who hold a Green Card (i.e., those who hold an unlimited residence visa, the so-called legal permanent residents). Memorandum from Donald F. McGahn II on Authoritative Guidance on Executive Order entitled "Protecting the Nation from Foreign Terrorist Entry into the United States" (Jan. 27, 2017), http://www.buffalo.edu/immigration-update/faculty-and-scholars.host.html/content/shared/www/immigration-update/travel-guidance-for-permanent-residents.detail.html.

[5] The United States Refugee Admissions Program (USRAP) is a refugee program that has been into force since 1980, following the enactment of the Refugee Act, which in turn incorporates the definition of "refugee" into federal immigration law, namely the Immigration and Nationality Act (the original version dates back to 1965 and has been amended several times). Prior to President Trump, no U.S. President had suspended the USRAP program in its entirety.

[6] Original version refers to: "on a case-by-case basis, and when in the national interest."

[7] California, Maryland, Massachusetts, Minnesota, New York, Oregon, and Washington.

[8] *Everson v. Board of Education*, 330 U.S. 1, 15 (1947). The Supreme Court held that the First Amendment provision according to which "Congress shall make no law for the recognition of any religion" contains a prohibition, binding on both the Federation and the States, against benefiting any religion to the exclusion of others, or giving one religion a preferential treatment over others.

[9] As mentioned, the Equal Protection Clause and the Due Process Clause are both contained, one after the other, in the Fifth Amendment; similar rules are also contained in the Fourteenth Amendment. The relationship between these two provisions is one of means to an end: The Due Process of Law is conceived as a protective tool of uniform regulation – equal protection – of certain fundamental rights of the individual: life, liberty, and property. Therefore, no limitation may be placed on those rights by the federal government (Fifth Amendment) or by the States (Fourteenth Amendment), without due process of law. What is meant by "due" is a question that must be resolved differently in relation to the type of procedure: Whether criminal, civil, administrative, or legislative. In the specific case of admission procedures, at the heart of these types of proceedings, there is, however, a minimum nucleus common to all of them: The procedure must be "fair," we say "equitable"; and "fair" is that procedure allowing the interested parties to present their reasons before an authority open to listening, that is, obliged to take those reasons as a founding element, together with other elements, of the decision. See Henry J. Friendly, *Some Kind of Hearing*, 94 U. Pa. L. Rev. 1267–1317 (1975).

[10] 8 U.S.C. § 1152(a)(1)(A).

[11] 8 U.S.C. §§ 1158 and 1231(b)(3).

[12] 22 U.S.C. 6501.

[13] *State of Washington v. Donald J. Trump et al.*, 17-CV-00141-JLR (2017). The Court granted the appeal on February 3, 2017, ordering a federal-wide suspension of the executive order.

[14] Equivalent of *periculum in mora* in the Italian legal system. *Periculum in mora* refers to the risk of serious damage occurring if a given measure is not suspended.

[15] Equivalent of *fumus boni iuris* in the Italian legal system. The *fumus boni iuris* indicates the probability of success on the merits.

[16] In fact, the force of the travel ban 1.0 harmed the plaintiffs (the States), insofar as immigrants residing (not permanently) in their territories would have suffered a limitation of their rights to work, to education, to freedom of economic initiative, to the right to carry out their private and family life, and to freedom of movement.

[17] Sabrina Siddiqui, *Travel Ban: US Temporarily Suspends Order as Trump Derides Judge*, The Guardian (Feb. 4, 2017), https://www.theguardian.com/us-news/2017/feb/04/so-called-judge-donald-trump-attacks-decision-to-halt-travel-ban.

[18] This is the federal court of appeals which has jurisdiction over appeals from judgments made by the District Court for the Western District of Washington (the first instance court in this case).

[19] The plenary power doctrine took shape in the late nineteenth century with the Supreme Court decision *Chae Chan Ping v. United States*, 130 U.S. 581 (1889). According to this doctrine, in matters of immigration, the politically sensitive powers (not only the Executive but also the Legislature) enjoy a sort of blank check, being able to regulate the issue in the manner that seems most politically expedient to them. The 1889 decision, therefore, greatly restricts the scope of the courts' review in immigration matters, which must limit themselves to applying the rational basis test. Indeed, the plenary powers doctrine has not been applied by the Court for several decades. See Steve Vladeck, *What's Missing from Constitutional Analyses of Donald Trump's Muslim Immigration Ban*, Just Security (Dec. 10, 2015), https://www.just-security.org/28221/missing-constitutional-analyses-donald-trumps-muslim-immigration-ban/, who points out that the last application, prior to the travel ban affair, was in *Mathews v. Diaz*, 426 U.S. 67 (1976).

[20] *Washington v. Trump*, 17-35105 (9th Circ. 2017).

[21] Vladeck, *supra* note 19, even before the entry into force of the first ban, claimed that such a measure violated both the Free Exercise Clause of the First Amendment – because it discriminated against Muslims on the basis of religious belief – and the Establishment Clause, a provision also implicitly contained in the First Amendment – because the state power disfavored people of Islamic religious orientation, thus favoring others who belong to another creed.

[22] Exec. Order No.13780, 82 Fed. Reg. 13209 (Mar. 6, 2017).

[23] In this way, the second version of the travel ban incorporates the clarification that, in relation to the first version, was made by the White House authoritative guidance.

[24] The removal of Iraq from the list of countries covered by the ban had been recommended by the Defense Secretary, Jim Mattis. He had expressed concern that if Iraq was left among the countries covered by the ban, it could jeopardize U.S.–Iraqi cooperation in the fight against the Islamic State.

[25] Indeed, in the appeals filed against travel ban 1.0, it was pointed out that the ad infinitum limitation of the ability to admit Syrian refugees was particularly problematic in light of the Due Process Clause.

[26] *State of Hawaii v. Donald Trump*, CV. NO. 17-00050 DKW-KSC. (D. Haw. 2017).

[27] *Hawaii v. Trump*, 859 F.3d 741 (9th Cir. 2017).

[28] *International Refugee Assistance Project v. Trump*, No. 17-cv-00361 (D. Md. 2017). The appeal was filed by six individuals and three associations of people of Islamic religion.

[29] *International Refugee Assistance Project v. Trump*, 857 F3.d 554 (4th Cir. 2017).

[30] The Lemon test originates from the case, decided by the federal Supreme Court, *Lemon v. Kurtzman*, 403 U.S. 602 (1971). This is a test aimed at evaluating the respect, on the part of political power, of the Establishment Clause. In particular, in order to be neutral toward religion, a measure (law, executive order, or any other act of a public authority) must: Have a secular purpose (purpose prong); not have as its primary effect that of favoring or disadvantaging a particular religion (effect prong); not excessively involve public power in religious matters (entanglement prong).

[31] *Trump v. Int'l Refugee Assistance Project*, 582 U.S. ____ (2017).

[32] Effective until September 24, 2017, as subject to a sunset clause. Exec. Order 13780, 82 Fed. Reg. 13,209 (Mar. 9, 2017).

[33] Proclamation No. 9645, 82 Fed. Reg. 45161 (Sept. 24, 2017).

[34] Which will then be removed from the list by Proclamation No. 9723, 83 Fed. Reg. 15937 (Apr. 10, 2018).

[35] This change was introduced following a consultation by the Department of Security with the intelligence community. The latter had recommended the introduction of an element that would make it possible to reduce restrictions. In fact, some entries from so-called high-risk countries could even have been functional for a better knowledge of useful information for the fight against terrorism and other threats to national security.

[36] The same plaintiffs who had appealed the travel ban 2.0 in the Hawaiian jurisdiction asked the District Court, and were granted, permission to renew their complaints (as permitted by Article 65 of the Federal Code of Civil Procedure), adapting their appeal to the new version of the travel ban.

[37] *Hawaii v. Trump*, 265 F. Supp. 3d 1140, 1148 (D. Haw. 2017).

[38] *Id.* at 1145: "The President, in issuing the Executive Order, exceeded the scope of the authority delegated to him by Congress" as the ban "runs afoul of other provisions of the [Immigration and Nationality Act (INA), specifically 8 U.S.C. § 1152] that prohibit nationality-based discrimination."

[39] *Hawaii v. Trump*, 17-17168, 2017 WL 5343014 (9th Cir. 2017).

[40] With a petition for certiorari.

[41] *Trump v. Hawaii*, 585 U.S. ____ (2018). The majority opinion was written by Chief Justice Roberts and Justices Alito, Gorsuch, Kennedy, and Thomas concurred (Kennedy and Thomas also each write their own concurring opinion). Justice Sotomayor delivered a dissenting opinion (joined by Justice Ginsburg), and another dissenting opinion was delivered by Justice Breyer, joined by Justice Kagan.

[42] More precisely, the Court considers the measure as "plausibly related to the Government's stated objective."

[43] *Trump v. Hawaii*, 585 U.S. ____ (2018) (Kennedy, J., concurring).

[44] *Trump v. Hawaii*, 585 U.S. ____ (2018) (Sotomayor, J., dissenting). On the use of national security to shield Executive's wrongdoings, but regarding the different topic of state secrecy in the context of extraordinary renditions, see Arianna Vedaschi, *The Dark Side of Counter-Terrorism:* Arcana Imperii *and* Salus Rei Publicae, 66 Am. J. Comp. L. 877 (2018).

[45] Sotomayor cited Trump's election campaign, statements posted on the White House website, messages via Twitter, and the fact that, despite the (negative) media prominence his statements about Muslims caused, the President never retraced his steps. *Trump v. Hawaii*, 585 U.S. ____ (2018) (Sotomayor, J., dissenting).

[46] The term is taken from a practice sometimes used in the United States during elections. It is an operation aimed at designing electoral districts in such a way as to favor a given party. In clearer terms, the constituencies are structured to bring together portions of the territory that are ideologically cohesive (even if, perhaps, geographically distant or which, in any case, give rise to a jagged shape to the boundaries of the electoral colleges). The term derives from the name of Elbridge Gerry – governor of Massachusetts under whose administration, in 1812, a law was passed applying this practice – and from the word "salamander" (which evokes the shape, sometimes tortuous, that such constituencies often end up taking).

[47] 323 U.S. 214 (1944). "Today's holding is all the more troubling given the stark parallels between the reasoning of this case and that of Korematsu v. United States, 323 U.S. 214 (1944)."

[48] This is a standard of judgment whereby the Court does not limit itself to examining the not manifest unreasonableness of a measure adopted by the public authorities (as happens, instead, in the test of reasonableness), but goes on to assess whether the public interest pursued is "important" and whether the measures are "substantively related" to that interest. See *Craig v. Boren*, 429 U.S. 190 (1976).

[49] This refers to the most stringent standard of judgment that the Court can adopt in assessing the constitutionality of a measure. When applying strict scrutiny, the Court verifies the existence of a "compelling interest" that makes the adoption of that measure absolutely necessary. In addition, there must be no less intrusive means of achieving the objective pursued. See *United States v. Carolene Products Co.*, 304 U.S. 144 (1938).

[50] According to Justice Sotomayor, the ban "is 'divorced from any factual context from which we could discern a relationship to legitimate state interests,' and [...] the policy is 'inexplicable by anything but animus'." *Trump v. Hawaii*, 585 U.S. ____ (2018) (Sotomayor, J., dissenting).

[51] *Trump v. Hawaii*, 585 U.S. ____ (2018) (Breyer, J., dissenting).

[52] It should be recalled that the Supreme Court had lifted the suspension order and, therefore, the ban was currently effective in the United

States, which allowed the evaluation of its practical performance. The two dissenting justices pointed out that it does not seem that a careful case-by-case evaluation is applied, to the point that the number of foreigners from the States subject to the ban who have been let into the United States is very low.

[53] This Proclamation removes Chad from the list of restricted countries.

[54] The Supreme Court, confirming the previous ruling of the District Court of California by an extremely concise order (Order No. 594 U.S., August 24, 2021 pending the case of *Biden v. Texas et al.*), has suspended one particular side of the measure by which the Biden Administration had removed the executive orders adopted by Trump in the field of immigration and has suspended it until such time as the Administration itself will be able to demonstrate "not arbitrary nor capricious" that side of that measure. To be exact, the Court has ruled the revival of the program brought forward by Trump after a special negotiation with the Mexican government, the so-called Remain in Mexico program, regarding asylum seekers. In doing so, the Court has inevitably ended up dipping its spoon into the bowl of foreign policy, where the Supreme Court has always said and repeated – most recently in *Kiobel v. Royal Dutch Petroleum Co.*, 569 U.S. 108 (2013) – that the intervention of the courts should be "particularly wary of impinging on the discretion of the legislative and executive branches in managing foreign." The broad deference shown by the Court toward Trump seems, therefore, to have reversed into its opposite toward the new Administration.

[55] Peter J. Spiro, *Trump v. Hawaii, International Decisions,* 113 Am. J. Int. L. 109, 113 (2019) states that the Supreme Court's decision of June 2018 "normalized the Trump Presidency before the Court."

[56] Breyer underlined that "[a]n examination of publicly available statistics also provides cause for concern. The State Department reported that during the Proclamation's first month, two waivers were approved out of 6,555 eligible applicants. [...] That number [...], when compared with the number of pre-Proclamation visitors, accounts for a miniscule percentage of those likely eligible for visas." *Trump v. Hawaii*, 585 U.S. ____ (2018) (Breyer, J., dissenting).

[57] Sotomayor stated that "...a reasonable observer would readily conclude that the Proclamation was motivated by hostility and animus toward the Muslim faith" and that "the words of the President and his advisers create the strong perception that the Proclamation is contaminated by impermissible discriminatory animus against Islam and its followers." *Trump v. Hawaii*, 585 U.S. ____ (2018) (Sotomayor, J., dissenting).

[58] According to Sotomayor, "courts must take care not to engage in "any judicial psychoanalysis of a drafter's heart of hearts". *Id.*

[59] However, the doctrine underlines how the introduction of countries with a non-Muslim majority can be seen as an operation merely aimed at diverting attention from the criticism that the discriminatory intent of the ban was emerging. See Mark Tushnet, *Trump v. Hawaii: 'This President'*

and the National Security Constitution, 2018 Sup. Ct. Rev. 1, 4, talking about "attempt to put lipstick on the pig."

[60] Presidential Statement on Recent Executive Order Concerning Extreme Vetting (Jan. 29, 2017), https://id.usembassy.gov/president-donald-j-trump-statement-regarding-recent-executive-order-concerning-extreme-vetting/.

[61] Proclamation 8693, 76 Fed. Reg. 44751 (July 24, 2011). Paul Owen, *Barack Obama Breaks Silence on Trump Presidency to Condemn Migration Ban*, The Guardian (Jan. 30, 2017), https://www.theguardian.com/us-news/2017/jan/30/barack-obama-travel-ban-statement-protests-trump.

[62] Policies relating to border controls and asylum as well as to the fight against illegal immigration are not only specific to each State but are also functional, in the United States, to the elimination of internal border controls. These policies are, by their very nature, variable in relation to the changing of a number of factors, and two of them in particular: One is the level of unemployment and/or labor supply in the country; the other is the varying difficulty of border surveillance. Whenever the level of unemployment in the country has risen above a certain limit, or the supply of labor has dropped dramatically, or when border surveillance, due to exceptional circumstances, has presented such shortcomings as to constitute a serious threat to public order and internal security, the U.S. government has introduced measures to contain immigration: Obama has done so, Bush Jr. has done so, Theodore Roosevelt has done so in the past, other Presidents have done so – autonomously or through Congress. In all these cases, however, it would be improper to discuss "precedents" with respect to the immigration policies pursued by Donald Trump. If it is legitimate to speak of "precedents," the reference – if anything – should be made, with all due reservations, to the Chinese Exclusion Act of 1882, which blocked the immigration of the Chinese for 10 years and should be made to the Immigration (Johnson-Reed) Act of 1924, a law that imposed a block on immigration from the whole of Asia, except for the Philippines and Japan. However, the differences are so striking that, on closer inspection, the reference is very difficult to make. The two laws of Congress just mentioned are in fact the expression of a policy of citizenship based on ethnic differences and carried out within a society steeped in racist prejudices. Samuel P. Huntington, Who Are We? The Challenges to American National Identity (2004). In 1889, the Supreme Court, in the case *Chae Chan Ping v. United States*, 130 U.S. 581, affirmed the constitutionality of the Chinese Exclusion Act because, as Justice Stephen J. Field stated, since the Chinese belonged to a different race, it seemed "impossible for them to assimilate" and "they remained strangers, isolating themselves in their communities and remaining bound to the customs and habits of their country." If not contained, Justice Field reasoned, this "Oriental invasion" would pose "a threat to our civilization." The same is to be said with respect to the Immigration Act of 1924. On the contrary, in the case of the three travel bans adopted by Trump through as many exec-

utive orders, these are measures to protect public order and internal security that, according to the Supreme Court itself, have nothing to do (but will it be true?) with racial or cultural bias.

[63] Peter J. Spiro, *Trump v. Hawaii, International Decisions*, 113 Am. J. Int. L. 109, 114 (2019) (underlining how the decision reaffirms the so-called plenary powers doctrine).

10 The Attempt Made to Tightly Seal the South-West Border: The Mexican Wall

The practical implementation of the idea of building a wall along the border with Mexico with the purpose of stopping illegal immigration had to face political scrutiny, carried out by Congress and public opinion, as well as judicial scrutiny, that is to say scrutiny on compliance with the Constitution and other laws. The latter was carried out by multiple levels of courts, part of both state and federal jurisdiction.

The Executive Order on Border Security under Examination at Congress

We have already mentioned how Trump championed a restrictive policy in matters of immigration. One of the promises on which Donald Trump based is electoral campaign in 2015–2016 was – as we have seen – to stop illegal immigration and, in his vision, to stop criminality coming from beyond the border, and specifically from Mexico, by building a wall along the U.S. Southern border.[1] On a wave of propaganda to promote his election as President, the candidate Donald Trump announced to his electors that the necessary expenses for building the wall would have been paid by the Mexican government.[2] Similarly as he did with the travel ban, on January 25, 2017, only a few days after the beginning of his mandate at the White House, President Trump signed Executive Order No. 13767,[3] titled: "Border Security and Immigration Enforcement Improvements." With this Act, the new Administration committed to raising a wall,[4] more than 1850 km long, between the United States and its "dangerous" neighbor (in the mind of Donald Trump), so as to discourage possible clandestine crossings. With regard to financial aspects, the order in question mentioned already existing federal funds, not specifying which centers of imputation would be used to start these very expensive works nor was it specified which procedures would be used in order to make the (presumed) funds available. On the delicate matter of the works' financing, the Trump Administration was probably hoping to find a favorable compromise with the then Mexican President, Enrique Peña Nieto, who was invited to Washington on January 27, 2017, that is, two days after the order was signed. However, due to the unwise declarations of President Trump, who the day before the meeting with the Mexican head of State, in one of his typical outbursts, announced he would "unload" the whole cost of the wall on Mexico, by imposing a 20% tax on imported goods, President Peña Nieto instantly cancelled the meeting with Donald Trump[5] and indeed made clear that his country would not pay for the border wall.

After this, in the intent of finding the necessary funds among the federal budget items for 2019, between the end of 2017 and the first months of 2018, President Trump would start informal negotiations with the members of Congress, but these would soon turn out to be unproductive, since both on the Democratic and Republican side, clear opposition emerged against the Executive's proposal. To this regard, it should be pointed out that, regardless of their political side, among the arguments used by those who opposed the President's policy of contrasting criminality by controlling immigration, there was the lack of reasonability, given the evident disproportion between the means adopted and the purpose intended. In clearer terms, the awareness was emerging that the wall, that is, a physical barrier, along the border between the two countries, was not the best option to solve problems relating to immigration control, which were also, in the mind of Trump, problems relating to the control of criminality. On the contrary, and this is worth noting, according to the opponents, it would have been best to consider less "invasive" means, that is, less radical but more effective, as, for example, strengthening the border control and using technology in order to trace possible illegal activity of people intending to cross the border.[6] In this context, in March 2018, the Congress, gathered to vote the federal budget forecast for 2019, allocated 1.6 billion dollars for the building of infrastructure generically directed at border protection. However, no reference was made to the wall that Donald Trump was so insistently asking for. Deeming the sum inadequate, Trump pushed for an amendment to the budget law so as to add as many as 5 billion dollars to border security and immigration enforcement. Under the procedural aspect, this proposal was formalized in October 2018 when some Republican members of the House of Representatives introduced a bill for the allocation of additional funds (supplemental appropriation bill).[7] In December 2018, Congress voted the Consolidated Appropriation Act, whose text, at least in the approved version, did not include the funds requested by the President and expected from the aforementioned amendment. Faced with the decision of the Legislature, Donald Trump threatened to veto the whole budget law.[8] So began an exhausting battle between the presidency and the legislative power, which, due to the freezing of the funds, inevitably resulted in blocking the entire federal Administration. In order to avoid the paralysis of the Administration apparatus, the Congress attempted to mediate by proposing temporary allocations, but the President kept to his intransigent line and denied approval: What followed was a shutdown.[9]

The contrast between the executive and legislative power would worsen with changes in the political situation. In fact, during the mid-term elections held in November 2018, the Democrats won the majority at the House of Representatives; consequently, from January 2019,[10] the clash between the President and Congress would exacerbate, with the former being convinced of the necessity to build a wall to protect the Southern border from "Mexican criminality," and the latter – the House of Representatives being at the time driven by Democrats – opposed to the idea of financing the structure with federal funds. Several members of Congress, both Democrat and Republican, strongly opposed the shutdown strategy calling it unfair, as it was intended to bend the legislative power to the President's will, by means of "taking hostage" hundreds of thousands of staff members in federal agencies.[11]

In the midst of protests, the longest shutdown in American history was then relieved thanks to the approval of a provisional measure that temporarily allowed allocation of the funds necessary for the administrative work to restart (stopgap bill). In particular, thanks to this bill, which quickly became a statute, starting from January 25, 2019, the shutdown would be interrupted for three weeks, the time necessary for members of Congress, Republicans as well as Democrats, to find an agreement both on the budget and the issue of funds to be allocated to government's policies on immigration and, more specifically, the possible building of the border wall.

The situation was finally unjammed on February 15, 2019, when President Trump signed the Consolidated Appropriations Act[12] allocating 1.37 billion dollars for the building of the wall in the area of Rio Grande Valley. However, believing the wall required greater financial support, Trump also declared the state of emergency[13] on the basis of the National Emergency Act (NEA) 1976.[14]

Within the declaration of emergency, the claim was that the Southern border of the United States served as a dangerous doorway for the entrance of criminals trafficking illegal drugs and other transnational criminal activities. Additionally, at a practical level, the President pointed out that the U.S. was in the difficult situation of having to prepare places suitable for detaining subjects who had been arrested on federal territory and waiting to be expelled. This was the basis on which the Trump Administration claimed the need for a greater effort, mostly in financial terms, to confront a crisis that, in the opinion of the Administration, represented a real national emergency. In order to face situations of national emergency, the President has indeed the power to reallocate federal funds that are not destined to other expenses, as long as he clearly specifies the dispositions by which he was intending to act.[15] In other words, even in the context of an emergency, the President must act on the basis (and within the limits) of the power granted to him by Congress. A presidential action that is unchecked by the "support" previously given by Congress[16] would violate the so-called Appropriation Clause, established in Article 1, Section IX, of the Constitution. According to this clause, the necessary funds cannot be drawn from the Treasury and are instead made available thanks to a specific financing allocated by law.[17]

In this setting, the White House published a factsheet, where the budget centers were indicated, that is, the means by which to cover the costs for the building of the wall. First of all, according to the "guidelines" given by the Trump Administration: 601 million dollars were to come from the Department of Treasury Forfeiture Fund, a fund set up by law,[18] periodically authorized by Congress and financed with money coming from law enforcement operations (e.g., fines, confiscated funds, etc.)

It should be pointed out, incidentally, that the use of this part of the budget does not require any declaration of emergency. Similarly, there is no requirement to act in the context of a state of emergency in order to draw the additional 2.5 billion dollars allocated on the basis of Section 284 of Title 10 U.S. Code.[19] In particular, this provision allows the Secretary of Defense to use federal funds to contrast drug trafficking activities and/or other similar transnational crimes; so, among the operations that the Secretary of Defense can finance, there is explicit mention of the construction of roads and fencing and the installing of lighting systems in order to obstruct the routes of drug trafficking used to cross the borders of the United States. Finally, and this is the only part of the budget justified by the declaration of emergency, another 3.6 billion dollars were to be acquired by the federal budget financed by taxpayers and, specifically, by the budget items set for civil infrastructure. According to Section 2808 of Title 10 U.S. Code,[20] these funds can be used by the Department of Defense for constructions having a military purpose, even without an ad hoc legislative attribution, as long as there has been a previous declaration of emergency by the President. Therefore, the 3.6 billion dollars "covered" by Section 2808 would be the portion of federal funds the use of which would have been justified by the controversial declaration of emergency.

Over the actual existence of a situation of emergency, there was an immediate clash between the President and Congress. The difference in perception became clear when, on February 25, 2019, in an attempt to put an end to the state of emergency,[21] the Congress voted a joint resolution,[22] which the President promptly vetoed.[23] The Congress, with the Senate being prevalently Republican, could not find the two-thirds majority from each House, that is the quorum, as known, essential in order to override the President's veto. Consequently, notwithstanding the strenuous opposition of the House of Representatives, that had a democrat majority after the mid-term elections, the construction of the wall (or rather the extension of the wall that already existed) started in March 2019;[24] the works were indeed accelerated by the financial aid of private organization that had been encouraged by Trump to offer their contribution for the "cause."[25]

...and under the Courts Examination

Once Trump had scored his political victory, the clash over the construction of the wall was to move to the judicial side, to which some resorted seeing the interests threatened. The main argument used by the plaintiffs both in *Alvarez v. Trump*[26] and in *Sierra Club v. Trump*[27] was that of the violation of the so-called Appropriation Clause.

Before the courts, both of first and second instances, the plaintiffs claimed that the state of emergency, declared by the President, was simply an excuse and that it had been triggered only in order to avoid the legitimate obstruction of Congress, that was not persuaded by the President's policy on immigration control (seen as an instrument to contrast criminality) and that was opposed, as we have seen, to allocate federal funds to pay for the wall. [28] In their complaints, the non-existence of a war conflict was particularly emphasized, meaning the type of conflict that would have legitimated a declaration of the state of emergency and would allow to use federal funds for the construction of military infrastructure. In fact, Section 2808 of title 10 of the U.S. Code, the legal basis employed by Trump to use the available money for the building of the wall, grants the President the power to reallocate federal funds, whenever it becomes necessary to build military infrastructure in order to face a situation of emergency. Otherwise the "main route" to follow passes through Congress by asking the legislative power to consent to the allocation of the funds. In this case, according to the plaintiffs, there was no situation of emergency and, consequently, neither the legal backing necessary for the request of funds.

In *Alvarez*, the Trump Administration presented a sworn declaration to affirm that the amount allocated for the construction of the wall had nothing to do with the federal funds "covered" by the declaration of emergency. This argument was accepted by the Court. Consequently, with the interest to act no longer in place, the legal action was considered settled.

In *Sierra Club*, the competent court of first instance, as a precautionary measure, allowed the suspension,[29] given the good chances of success. The precautionary injunction was to be also confirmed by the Court of Appeals for the Ninth Circuit.[30] The decision, in fact, had been contested by Trump, based on the argument that the funds had been allocated because of "unforeseen needs," also (but not only) of military nature.

The argument used, about the occurring of unforeseen needs, did not however convince the judges of the Court of Appeals, because it seemed inconsistent with the President's firm intention of ascribing the funds only to the construction of the border wall, an intention that had been frequently made explicit, both during the dispute with Congress, and before the competent courts. As a consequence, starting from May 2019, the construction of the wall was interrupted.

The precautionary injunction of the Court of Appeals was however challenged by the Trump Administration before the Supreme Court. There, with a rather concise order adopted on July 26, 2019,[31] the Court accepted President Trump's request and resolved the thorny issue at a procedural level, pointing out that the plaintiffs had no reason to act[32] against the Trump Administration. To put it more bluntly, having found a lack of motive in the plaintiffs' appeal,[33] the Supreme Court did not decide on the matter. After the Court's ruling, the Trump Administration ordered for the works to start again.

In the meantime, in the lower courts, the judgement on the merit was being celebrated, at least for Sierra Club.[34] The court of first instance found a violation of the Appropriation Clause and consequently of the principle of separation of powers, and therefore considered the President's action as unconstitutional.[35] The decision of first instance was later confirmed in second instance by the Court of Appeals for the Ninth Circuit where the Trump Administration had promptly challenged the decision of first instance.[36]

On this occasion too, matters were taken to the Supreme Court: President Trump filed a request for certiorari asking to reconsider the case. The Supreme Court, having accepted to rule on the matter,[37] suspended the procedure and postponed the hearings that had been already planned, in consideration of the determinations of the newly elected President Biden. Indeed, at the beginning of 2021, by putting an end to the state of emergency declared by Donald Trump because of the "Mexican threat,"[38] Joseph Biden ordered the suspension of the construction of the border wall and, what's more, announced that the lawfulness of the financing methods and procedures for the construction needed to be verified.

Notes

[1] According to the Washington Post, Trump mentioned the issue as many as 190 times during his first campaign. Fact Checker, *More Than Two Years Later, Trump's Wall Remain Unbuilt*, Washington Post (Sept. 6, 2019), https://www.washingtonpost.com/politics/2019/09/06/more-than-two-years-later-trumps-wall-remains-unbuilt/. Indeed, the wall would be a "completion" of a work already begun. In fact, a border separation barrier already existed for about 1000 km, started by President Clinton in 1993 and expanded by President G.W. Bush in 2006. Trump's action would therefore complete the remaining km (about 1850, the border between Mexico and the U.S. being 3100 km long), given that for 250 km a natural barrier extends.

[2] Mia Jankowicz, *A Timeline of Unfulfilled Promises Trump Made about His Border Wall, a Cornerstone of His 2016 Campaign which Has Faded from View in 2020*, Insider (Sept. 6, 2020), https://www.businessinsider.com/timeline-of-president-trumps-unfulfilled-border-wall-promises-2020-9?IR=T; Gary Reich, *Hitting a Wall? The Trump Administration Meets Immigration Federalism*, 48 J. Federalism 372 (2018).

[3] Exec. Order No.13767 82 Fed. Reg. 8793 (Jan. 25, 2017).

[4] To complete the barrier of about 1000 km already erected under the Clinton and Bush Jr. Administrations. See *supra* note 1.

[5] *Mexico: We Will Not Pay for Trump Border Wall*, BBC News (Jan. 26, 2017), https://www.bbc.com/news/world-us-canada-38753826.

[6] Lisa Mascaro, *Trump Wants a Border Wall, but Few in Congress Want to Pay for It*, The Times (Apr. 24, 2017), https://www.latimes.com/politics/la-na-pol-border-wall-shutdown-20170424-story.html.

[7] Specifically, the reference is to the Build the Wall, Enforce the Law Act 2018, H.R. 7059–115th Congress (2017–2018), to be included in the Consolidated Appropriations Act 2019.

[8] On the use of the veto power, see Giuseppe F. Ferrari, *L'esperienza statunitense*, in *Il Presidente della Repubblica* 489 (Massimo Luciani & Mauro Volpi eds., 1997).

[9] As is well known, the government shutdown is a procedure provided for by the Antideficiency Act 1884 (Pub. L. 97-258, 96 Stat. 923) that allows the shutdown of agencies – except those "involving the safety of human life or the protection of property" – when there is no financial coverage for them by Congress in the budget bill. The closure of the agencies causes the suspension of the payment of salaries of those who are employed and the blocking of their activities. The shutdown in question involved nine federal departments (with related agencies), with approximately 800,000 employees, placed on furlough and lasted from December 22, 2018, to January 25, 2019.

[10] That is, to coincide with when the newly elected members of Congress take office.

[11] Jonathan Chait, *If Trump Gets a Ransom to End the Shutdown, He'll Do It Again and Again*, Intelligencer (Jan. 23, 2019), https://nymag.com/intelligencer/2019/01/trump-ransom-shutdown-do-it-again-hostage-negotiation.html, in which are reported the words of the Democratic Senator Chuck Schumer.

[12] Pub. L. 116–6.

[13] Proclamation No. 9844,84 Fed. Reg. 4949 (Feb. 15, 2019).

[14] Pub. L. 94–412, 90 Stat. 1255. On presidential emergency powers, Mark Tushnet, *Can the President Declare a National Emergency to Build the Wall?*, Constitutioncenter.org (Jan. 10, 2019), https://constitutioncenter.org/interactive-constitution/podcast/can-the-president-declare-a-national-emergency-to-build-the-wall.

[15] "The provisions of law under which he proposes that he [...] will act." National Emergencies Act, 50 U.S.C § 1601-1651.

[16] Kim L. Scheppele, *Trump's Non-Emergency Emergency (Part I)*, Verfassungsblog (Feb. 15, 2019), https://verfassungsblog.de/trumps-non-emergency-emergency/. See also Jacqueline Lewis, *The Executive's Power of the Purse in National Emergency: The President's Plan to Poach Defense Funds to Build the Wall*, 34 Geo. Immigr. L. J. 825 (2020).

[17] "No Money shall be drawn from the Treasury, but in Consequence of Appropriations made by Law."

[18] Department of the Treasury Forfeiture Fund 31 U.S.C. § 9705(g)(4)(B).

[19] Support for counterdrug activities and activities to counter transnational organized crime. 10 U.S.C. § 284.

[20] Construction authority in the event of a declaration of war or national emergency U.S.C. § 2808(a).

[21] Power granted to it by Section 202 of the NEA, which states that a state of emergency may come to an end either by a joint resolution of Congress or by presidential proclamation.

[22] H.J. Res. 46, 116th Cong. (2019–2020).

[23] Note that the original version of the NEA provided that the President could not veto the congressional resolution ending the state of emergency. However, the Supreme Court, in *INS v. Chadha*, 462 U.S. ____ (1983), later declared this provision unconstitutional, stating that the President should be given the ability to exercise his veto power over these types of acts as well. Thus, Congress's power of control over the declaration of an emergency under the NEA is greatly debased, since the only way it can override the President's decision is to find a two-thirds majority of each chamber to override any veto.

[24] Extending, in all, for 499 miles (about 803 km).

[25] Specifically, the organization called "We Build the Wall" organization has been involved in the construction of several miles of wall, funding itself through fundraising.

[26] This is an appeal filed on February 15, 2019, by several U.S. citizens, who owned property on the U.S.–Mexico border, before the United States District Court for the District of Columbia.

[27] Appeal filed by Sierra Club, a California environmental organization, on February 19, 2019, in the District Court for the Northern District of California.

[28] The plaintiffs cite the case of *Youngstown v. Sawyer*, 343 U.S. 579 (1952). This is a case, which occurred before the NEA was passed, in which the Supreme Court declared unconstitutional an executive order of President Truman, who had used the Commander-in-Chief Clause of the Constitution to seize certain enterprises to deal with the Korean War, in order to overcome the prohibition of Congress to authorize such an operation by law. The Supreme Court had sustained that the recourse to the emergency had been merely instrumental in evading the denial of Congress. Luca P. Vanoni, *Il muro di Trump tra emergency powers e separazione dei poteri*, Quaderni costituzionali (2019); see also Andy Carr, *The Border Wall Emergency Declaration – Power Grab or Culmination of Expansive Presidential Authority?*, 2019 Ne. U.L. Rev. 1.

[29] *Sierra Club v. Trump*, 19-cv-00892-HSG. (D. N. Cal. 2019).

[30] *Sierra Club v. Trump*, 929 F.3d 670 (9th Cir. 2019).

[31] *Trump v. Sierra Club*, 140 S. Ct. 1 (Mem.), 204 L.Ed.2d 1170 (2019).

³² The Court found that the plaintiffs "had no cause of action."

³³ Justices Ginsburg, Sotomayor, and Kagan dissented from the majority opinion; however, since this is an order, there is no opinion stating the reasons for the dissent.

³⁴ As noted above, in the *Alvarez* case, the appellants had instead waived their appeal.

³⁵ *Sierra Club v. Trump*, No. 4:19-cv-00892 (2019); WL 2715422 (N.D. Cal., 2019).

³⁶ *Sierra Club v. Trump*, 963 F.3d 874 (9th Cir. 2020). This judgment also decided another appeal, filed by California and 20 other States, but which had been dismissed in the first instance.

³⁷ *Trump v. Sierra Club*, 141 S. Ct. 618 (2020).

³⁸ Proclamation No. 10142, 86 Fed. Reg. 7225 (Jan. 20, 2021). This Proclamation terminates the emergency.

⁶⁴ In this vein, see the dissenting opinions in the aforementioned *Korematsu* case. In that context, Justice Murphy, while acknowledging the need for special deference to the Executive when national security is at stake, emphasized that "it is essential that there be definite limits to [the government's] discretion," because "[i]ndividuals must not be left impoverished of their constitutional rights on a plea of military necessity that has neither substance nor support." 323 U.S. 214 (1944), at 234 (Murphy, J., dissenting). Justice Jackson, moreover, stated how the majority's decision, in favor of governmental policy, turns out to be "a far more subtle blow to liberty than the promulgation of the order itself," since, even with the change of a new Executive, the Court would continue to tolerate such policies. *Id.* at 245–246.

11 The Executive and Legislative Power in the Age of Trump

At this point, before continuing our analysis, it is worth saying something about the dynamics of the debate between Trump and Congress, as well as those between the two parties and their behavior inside Congress.

Let us start from a premise. Generally speaking, the President and Congress are engaged in a relationship that swings between periods of serenity and others of tearing conflict, but the relationship endures because the Constitution requires for neither of them to become separated from the other. We can use a botanic metaphor again and say that between the President and Congress, there is a kind of antagonistic symbiosis, being the two connected as they are, by a process of mutual influence, or conditioned evolution, which, in turn, may favor the one to the detriment of the other.

This relationship, still incredibly complex, seemed to have reached its breaking point during Trump's mandate.

First of all, one thing is perfectly understood. The growing conflict between the legislative and executive power over the construction of the wall (or better, over the policies aimed at fighting organized crime through the control of immigration), which reached the extreme point of a proclamation of national emergency, shows in all evidence the breakdown in the dialogue between the two powers, both of them forced, right from the beginning of the Trump experience, into a very unhappy marriage.

A closer look can allow us to be more precise and so to notice that one of the most evident anomalies of Trump's presidency, among the many that characterized it, was the continuous if not inherent dispute between the executive and legislative power; and this is true even for the first two years of Trump's mandate when his party had the majority in both the House of Representatives and the Senate – a situation known as "unified government." Here too, we can see that the two powers in no way enjoyed the typical time known as honeymoon period,[1] when Congress generally acts lovingly toward the President who can work "with the wind in the sails" blowing from the popular vote received just a few weeks or months prior.[2]

Then, what were the reasons for this anomaly? An answer can be found – as a recent study by G.C. Edwards[3] suggests – in the link between some elements that enter the scene starting from a basic concept. This concept, if looked at closely, is two-faced, and these two sides, just as the god Janus, look into opposite directions: One to the advantage of Trump and the other to his disadvantage. His advantage was that he was able to act, at least for a long period of his mandate, in a situation (as mentioned earlier) of unified government, that is, during the 115th Congress under Republican majority; this being a situation theoretically allowing him – given certain conditions – to cover the role of President as leader of Congress, which would be joined to the role, granted to him by the Constitution, of head of the Executive.

On the other hand, what went to Trump's disadvantage was the highly divisive character of the main points of his agenda, both for the public opinion and the political establishment: From immigration policies to his response to COVID-19, from global warming to ethnic relations and gender policies, and more.

How did the scales tip to his disadvantage? How can the continuous and permanent conflict with Congress be explained in other words? Why did a red-light flash most of the times that an initiative by Trump went through Congress, needing to be passed into law?

A clear and strong contribution to this came from the intolerance that Trump showed toward the Washington's politicking establishment, or better, Trump's mediocre abilities in the art of mediation and compromise, these being skills that are often essential in order to solve the delicate issues of a political agenda.[4] In other words, what certainly played against Trump was his total inability to "break," via the practice of persuasion, the compact democratic front, or to "re-gain" the "agitated" Republicans. One can consider, just as an ex-ample, the continuous threats that the President uttered anytime a member of Congress would deny their support; or consider the in-credibly harsh shouting matches with Nancy Pelosi, the Speaker of the House of Representatives.[5]

As well as this, let us say, "behavioral" element, one should con-sider Trump's political weakness, as a President elected in 2016 more by exclusion, that is, thanks to votes that were rather against Hillary Clinton than in his favor.[6] Neither should we neglect that the ham-mering rhetoric of the "Make America Great Again" slogan did not find an adequate and coherent application in any program of political action, if not in sporadic initiatives such as the Mexican border wall and the travel ban.

Besides these elements of personal nature, there were also "con-textual" elements, so to speak. One was the polarization of the polit-ical system, deriving from the strong divisiveness of the presidential agenda; and this polarization did not only create a greater distance between the two parties[7] but also created a rift across the Republican party itself, undermining its unity. In other words, this polarization united the Democrats and divided the Republicans. And this was made worse, for Trump, by the fact that during his first two years of presidency – 2017 and 2018 – the Republicans had the majority by only 47 seats at the House of Representatives and as few as 4 at the Senate.

This eventually meant that most times the President's initiatives would follow a course where they got stuck at Congress,[8] a course toward which the Democratic opposition pushed and that the Re-publican found not too painful. To put it more bluntly: Congress was for Trump like a thick layer of marble which was impossible for the President to perforate, if not on very rare occasions.

The epilogue of the whole story concerning the Mexican wall now becomes clear: Faced with the difficulty of finding the necessary funds for its construction, President Trump went as far as declaring a national emergency, which is surely not totally uncustomary in American history, though in this case, the declaration was used in order to bypass an internal institutional clash (between the legislative and executive powers). And perhaps this, rather than just an institutional clash, was a strictly political and doubly internal conflict, given, on the one hand, the fierce political polarization between Democrats and Republicans and, on the other, the unreliable support of the President's party.

The extreme complexity that marks the relation between the two branches in the Trump era is confirmed by the increasing tendency of the President to adopt acts that did not involve Congress in the ordinary governing practice. This trend became evident after the mid-term elections that, after autumn 2018, handed over to the Democrats, the House of Representatives.[9] In fact, the whole two years of the second half of the mandate were characterized by an inherent difficulty for the Administration, if not an actual incapacity, of bringing forward, following the normal institutional channels, any kind of legislative initiative in line with the agenda promoted during the electoral campaign; hence the ever increasing tendency to favor unilateral action,[10] displaying a plebiscitary approach to power, exasperated by the strong political polarization. An example of this unilateralism was the frequent use of executive orders, even on delicate subjects or issues of significant political contrast that were now instead exposed to an undeniable populist deviation; suffice it to mention the demagoguery displayed on the subject of immigration.

In the cases examined, the "escape" from Congress, in the President's perspective, had a positive outcome in the case of the travel ban; having the budget approved turned out instead less easy, when the Constitution, and in particular the Appropriation Clause, obstructed the President's action, to the point of making him declare the state of emergency, which basically meant "gambling" beyond the line of legality. Differently than in other cases, Congress did not block the President's action, and instead first expressed a doubt on the actual reality of an emergency situation to then contest it via a formal vote. Never had there been such a direct clash on a subject so delicate, as is the assessment of "stressful circumstances."[11]

To summarize on this last point: The declaration of emergency, which the President used in order to overcome the constitutional boundary that prevented him from accessing the necessary funds for the construction of the wall as it had been planned, was opposed by the Congress' resolution,[12] in turn blocked by the President's veto. Given the impossibility of reaching a two-thirds majority in the two branches of the legislative power,[13] which is the essential condition to have the veto removed, the clash between legislative and executive powers came to an end.

Incidentally, we should point out that whereas in the first two years of his mandate Trump refrained from exercising his power of veto (Article I, Section VII, cl.3, of the Constitution) in the last eighteen months, he did so as many as nine times.[14]

In light of this, it can be argued that, in Donald Trump's understanding, the presidential role is blatantly oriented, theoretically, to the unitary executive theory,[15] in its most extreme version. This approach was made clear, albeit never expressly declared, ever since his political campaign, when Trump the candidate reassured his voters explaining he would carry out his program even without the (necessary) cooperation of Congress (which instead, from a constitutional point of view, the President cannot avoid). And so he did, very frequently, every time he resorted to executive orders: Consider the travel ban and not only. In fact, the President went even further, by arguing for the unreviewability thesis, which would bar the courts from making pronouncements on the President's choices.

To sum up, Trump's presidency was characterized, on the one hand, by the attempt to make another step forward along the way of the constant widening of the role and powers of the Executive, an expansion that has been increasing at least since the second half of the twentieth century.[16] Trump's presidency was also characterized, on the other hand, as an attempt to blur the pivotal system of checks and balances, already deteriorated in its functioning. The latter – that is, the attempt to dismantle the already compromised system of checks and balances – is, without a doubt, the most dangerous of President Trump's legacies, given how it could gain the title of precedent, in theory, which a new President could decide to invoke.

The unitary executive theory has enjoyed remarkable success over the last century. However, the fact remains that its more radical version (the imperial executive theory) practiced by Trump over the four years of his mandate seems very hardly compatible both with the Constitution and with the checks and balances, which the Constitution itself has as its cornerstone.

Notes

[1] Giuseppe F. Ferrari, *President Trump and the Congress*, 2021 DPCE Online 909.

[2] Lawrence J. Grossback et al., *Comparing Competing Theories on the Causes of Mandate Perceptions*, 49 Am. J. Pol. Sc. 406 (2005).

[3] George C. Edwards III, *'Closer' or Context? Explaining Donald Trump's Relations with Congress*, 48 Pres. St. Q. 456 (2018).

[4] Richard Neustadt, *Presidential Power. The Politics of Leadership* (1960) according to whom the President's role is heavily based on bargaining, persuasion, and compromise.

[5] See, for example, the refusal to shake hands with the Speaker of the House of Representatives at the 2020 State of the Union address.

[6] See Edwards, *supra* note 3, at 458.

[7] In fact, it should be underlined that President Trump has obtained the support of the Democratic congressmen only in "borderline" situations, such as when, in January 2018, in order to avoid the shutdown threatened by Trump due to the harsh opposition with Congress on the DACA (Deferred Action for Childhood Arrivals) program on migration, the Democrats voted for a spending bill, which included a so-called fund-cutting amendment, certainly not appreciated by the Democrats. Despite the opening of the opposition, as it is known, the shutdown was then also declared (from January 20 to 22, 2018), due to the lack of agreement on the subjective scope of DACA.

[8] It should be remembered that, in the U.S. system, the two branches of Congress are not obliged to consider a proposal, although, as a matter of practice, presidential proposals are statistically less likely to be dropped.

[9] Stephen D. Ansolabehere & Jon C. Rogowski, *Unilateral Action and Presidential Accountability*, 50 Pres. St. Q. 129 (2020).

[10] Andrew Reeves & Jon C. Rogowsky, *Unilateral Action, Public Opinion and the Presidency*, 78 J. Pol. 137 (2016). William P. Barr, *The Role of the Executive*, 43 Harv. J.L. & Pub. Pol'y 605 (2019).

[11] This expression is borrowed from the work of Michel Rosenfeld, who defines emergency conditions as "times of stress." M. Rosenfeld, *Judicial Balancing in Times of Stress: Comparing the American, British and Israeli Approaches to the War on Terror*, 27 Cardozo. L. Rev. 2079 (2006).

[12] By a vote of 245 in favor and 182 against in the House of Representatives and 59 in favor to 41 in the Senate.

[13] The results of the vote were in the House of Representatives 248 in favor of the veto over-ride versus 181.

[14] Donald Trump: Vetoed Legislation, Ballotpedia, https://ballotpedia. org/Donald_Trump:_Vetoed_legislation.

[15] This theory was explicitly recalled during the Reagan presidency, but already enhanced in the early 1970s by Arthur Schlesinger, with his work on the so-called imperial presidency. Arthur M. Schlesinger, *The Imperial Presidency* (1973). See also Steven G. Calabresi et al., *The Unitary Executive: Presidential Power from Washington to Bush* (2008), according to whom the executive power, especially on matters of foreign policy, is the holder of a real empire; Samuel Alito, *Administrative Law: Presidential Oversight & the Administrative State*, 2001 Engage 11, which emphasizes that the President holds the Executive in its entirety. John P. Mackenzie, *Absolute Power: How the Unitary Executive Theory Is Undermining the Constitution* (2008); for a reconstruction on developments in unitary executive theory, criticisms of it, and its applications in recent presidencies, see Jeffrey Crouch et al., *The Unitary Executive Theory and President Donald Trump*, 47 Pol. Sci. Q. 561, 573 (2017).

[16] Since the 1980s, the theory of the unitary executive has even been explicitly referred to in some presidential acts. In 1987, President Reagan, in one of his statements, defined presidential authority as "head of a unitary executive branch." Presidential statement on Signing the Federal Debt Limit and Deficit Reduction Bill (Sept. 29, 1987), https://www.reaganlibrary.gov/ archives/speech/statement-signing-federal-debt-limit-and-deficit-reduction-bill. See also the expansion of the powers of the executive branch during the presidencies of G.H.W. Bush, especially in the context of the Gulf War, and G.W. Bush, in the context of the war on terror. Bush Jr., in particular, has repeatedly invoked the theory of the unitary executive to justify his powers, which have often encroached even in areas where the President does not have an explicitly recognized prerogative. This tendency is evident in the areas of mass surveillance, detention of terrorists or suspected terrorists at Guantánamo, and the use of military commissions. Notwithstanding the fact that it has formally criticized the policies of the Bush Administration on several occasions, not even the Obama Administration has shied away, on a practical level, from the expansionist thrusts of presidential powers, for example, initiating military operations without congressional authorization or continuing to tolerate those anti-terrorism measures – Guantánamo, military commissions, particularly aggressive mass surveillance – that characterized the G.W. Bush Administration.

12 A Blood-Drenched Offence to the Temple of Democracy: The Attack of the "Patriots" on Capitol Hill

Francis Fukuyama is probably right when he states that "many Trump supporters genuinely believe that Trump won a massive landslide and that the election was stolen from him by massive fraud. If you believe that, you would be angry and violent as well."[1] Yes, it is true, this opinion bears all the signs of being too reckless: The rioters, Fukuyama seems to be saying, are blameless. But, in reality, this opinion is more plausible than it at first appears. The mob – in reality, a rowdy, motley gang – who attacked Capitol Hill, the "temple" of American democracy, had no intention of attacking the democracy of their country, but instead thought they were defending it. Trump, having skillfully set in motion a "parallel" communication universe, in fact succeeded in convincing "his" people – the people who are the "true" Americans, the people who are "patriots" – that he, he and them, had won outright his second term in the White House, a victory that the Democrats had supposedly stolen under everyone's eyes. Trump's plan, for that matter barely disguised, was extremely devious: Using his supporters, whom he had convinced that they had to defend democracy, to "stop the steal," by actually attacking it.

This plan, which failed miserably (and fortunately) as evidence shows, was organized over two levels.

One the first level is set Trump's veiled but clear approval of acts of violence frequently perpetrated by the "patriots" on democratic institutions at state level,[2] already well before the storming of Capitol Hill. An example is what happened at Michigan State Capitol, on

April 30, 2020: A rabble of rioters, some of them armed, stormed into the seat of the local Legislature with the intent to prevent the extension of the lockdown ordered by the state governor.[3]

The second level comprises the oft-repeated statement by Trump that the Democrats, having manipulated vote counting operations in certain key States, thereby violated the crucial pivot of every democracy: The decisive value of elections. Hence Trump's incitement, implicit but perfectly clear, to react strongly against those who – according to him – were planning to betray democracy.

These two levels, already intertwined by their nature, combined with a third level: Trump's massive injection, in 2020, of conservative federal judges into the circuit courts of key States crucial in the upcoming presidential election. He thought these judges would be ready to support him – such was Trump's delusion – over eventual challenges pertaining to vote counts in their States.

This is the framework in which the assault on Capitol Hill finally came to a head on January 6, 2021.

It is thus no surprise that the House of Representatives, events having reached their breaking point, decided, on January 11, 2021, to put in motion impeachment proceedings against Donald Trump – by that time at the end of his term of office. Hence, the President was called before the Senate for his attempts to tamper with the mechanism of the democratic process.[4]

A Digression on Impeachment

Here it seems necessary, before proceeding further, to say a few words about this special impeachment process. Let us go one step at a time.

The "form" of government in the United States is "presidential," or better it is actually the prototype of this kind. The key element is that the Executive starts and ends not in Congress, but in the ballot urns; in other words, the Executive does not need the "confidence" of Congress, unlike in Italy, where there is a confidence relationship between the majority of the Houses of Parliament and the Executive. The Philadelphia Founders made the choice in favor of a monocratic

Executive, the President, elected for four years by the people originally by the double vote election system that however over time was
transformed into a direct election, due to the fact that the so-called
Presidential electors – the "Great Electors" – receive a binding mandate from the citizens.

Now, the fact that the Executive starts and ends in the urns has
two consequences: First, the President does not have the power to
dissolve Congress ahead of time, since the President/Chief Executive is not nominated/appointed by Congress but is instead elected by
the votes of the people; second, Congress cannot pass a motion of no
confidence in the Executive, for the very good reason that the Executive remains in place not on the basis of the confidence of Congress,
but thanks to the popular vote. This being the case, the only way
Congress has to force the President to resign (who, it bears repeating,
subsumes and serves two functions, which are distinct in parliamentary systems, those of head of State and of head of the Executive, and
is free of any form of responsibilities outside of those deriving from
his relationship with public opinion), is to make use of that irregular
remedy consisting in the impeachment process.

The complex impeachment proceeding starts when the President
has committed, at least according to the incrimination formulated by
the House of Representatives, one or other of the crimes of "treason,
bribery, or other high crimes and misdemeanors" (Article II, Section IV, of the Constitution). Regarding the meaning of those terms,
we can reliably refer to Gigliola Sacerdoti Mariani, eminent linguist,
translator, and expert on the American Constitution.[5] She notes that
the final part of Section IV, precisely where we find the words "treason, bribery and other high crimes and misdemeanors," was redrafted
several times before reaching its definitive version. Starting from the
first version which reads "malpractice or neglect of duty," then altered
by the Committee of Details to treason, bribery, or corruption that
then was reduced to treason or bribery by the Committee of Eleven.
An amendment was then proposed, adding maladministration to the
above two terms. That word "maladministration" was deemed too
vague (but maybe danger was discerned in a term implying blatantly
political judgements), so high crimes and misdemeanors against the

United States was preferred. In the final stage, the Committee of Style, who never made substantial changes – so as not to alter the substantial meaning of the text – eliminated the phrase "against the United States," deemed superfluous in terms of the understanding of the clause. In conclusion, Sacerdoti Mariani notes that the historical indications supplied the implicit and explicit motivations that the Philadelphia delegates adduced for their choices of form and of substance, which provide that in using the terms high crimes and misdemeanors, they primarily had in mind crimes against the State, such as the abuse of power or abuse of state secrets (or other analogous infringements).

Now, it is interesting to start with the word "maladministration." Sacerdoti Mariani writes that, in the end, it was not used in the context of conduct susceptible to impeachment because, probably, they descried the danger of a term that implied blatantly political judgements.

Some experts had in fact stated, at least initially, that the impeachment could be turned, over time, into an anomalous form of a vote of no confidence, along the lines of the practice existing in parliamentary systems. In reality, this hypothesis, which the Founding Fathers had already discerned and discarded, was rejected in the course of political history quite early, that is, from the time when President Andrew Johnson, who as the Vice President to Lincoln succeeded the latter after his assassination, was subjected to the impeachment trial for having violated the Tenure of Office Act, a law that aimed at limiting the presidential power of removing from office federal officials.

The truth is that Johnson was a President loathed by large part of Congress, and widely unpopular in the North of the country, for his blatantly racist ideas. And the historian Hans L. Trefousse is right when he comments that "the weakness of the case [. . .] convinced many that the charges were largely political, and that the violation of the Tenure of Office Act constituted neither a crime nor a violation of the Constitution but merely a pretext for Johnson's removal."[6]

This interpretation was asserted at that point as an established principle (no longer open to doubt) that impeachment did not consist of a way, albeit anomalous, to assert the President's political responsibility before Congress, by the same logic that is proper to the confidence relationship in parliamentary systems, but nor, for that matter, was it a way to remove a President however incompetent or disliked.[7]

Nevertheless, leaving outside the door the Johnson "case," the theory that in some way pairs impeachment and the vote of no confidence in the Executive climbs back in through the window in terms of the judgement delivered by the Senate. In this case, after the House of Representatives has deliberated whether or not the President's conduct falls within the parameter (within the "type," the legal experts would say) of "high crimes and misdemeanors" found in Section IV of Article I, and thus eventually drafted the indictment in the form of a resolution subdivided into articles, the Senate is called to judge the indictment.[8] It does so by deciding whether to remove or vice versa to keep the President in office. It is a matter of political expediency, and as such relatively independent of the conclusions drawn by the House of Representatives. The experience of the "cases" of Johnson (February 24, 1868–May 2, 1868), Clinton (December 18, 1998–February 12, 1999), and the first impeachment of Donald Trump (December 18, 2019–February 5, 2020) prove this point.

The fact is that on February 13, 2021, the Senate, with a large Republican majority, dismissed all charges against Trump. It is true, at stake was not the eventual removal from office of the President, seeing that the new President was already in office;[9] what was however at stake was nevertheless a political judgement on Trump, a judgement that was (not in the sense of proscribing his running again for the White House, for example, but quite the contrary) in the sense of acknowledging his credibility as possible future candidate for President in 2024. In other words, the decision by the Senate on whether or not Trump could remain in office as President had shifted, in this particular case, from a presidency that was by now over to a hypothetical, future presidency.

The Sword of Damocles Looms on the Horizon for Trump

Emerging unscathed from the Senate judgement, can Trump say he is shielded once and for all against all accusations from the House of Representatives and thus able – in theory – to run for the White House in 2024? Maybe not, maybe he is not shielded.

Here comes into play the Fourteenth Amendment, dated 1868 and still fully in force. As laid down in Section 3 of the Fourteenth Amendment: "No person shall ... hold any office, civil or military, under the United States, ... who, having previously taken an oath, as a member of Congress, or as an officer of the United States, ... shall have engaged in insurrection or rebellion against the same, or given aid or comfort to the enemies thereof."[10] Implicit in the words "insurrection" and "rebellion" is the reference to those who had fought for the Southern States, the Confederacy, during the American Civil War. In 1872, Congress by two thirds majority decided, in agreement with President Grant, not to implement this disposition in the case of the Confederates, passing a law of amnesty in their favor. On the death of the last of the original recipients of the provision, there thereby lapsed the amnesty but certainly not the provision itself. Notwithstanding it is true that the "ban" foreshadowed in Section III of the Fourteenth Amendment was subsequently applied at least once, in the case of Victor L. Berger (1919), a socialist former member of Congress due to his "neutralist" speeches just before the United States went to war in the First World War.[11]

The question to ask is thus as follows: Does Donald Trump's conduct during the days of the Capitol Hill riot really adhere to the details listed in the Insurrection Clause of the Fourteenth Amendment?

To answer this question, it is necessary to read the facts and charges listed in H. Res. 24 in light of the Fourteenth Amendment. Congress can do it at every moment until the possible re-election of Donald Trump or also in the days following his inauguration into the White House assuming, without conceding, that he intends to run for the presidency and is able to do so pursuant to the rules of the Constitution.

Notes

[1] *Stanford Scholars React to Capitol Hill Takeover*, Stanford News (Jan. 6, 2021), http://news.stanford.edu/2021/01/stanford-scholars-react-capitol-hill-takeover/.

[2] Ryan Goodman, Mari Dugas & Nicholas Tonckens, *Incitement Timeline: Year of Trump's Actions Leading to the Attack on the Capitol*, Just Security (Jan. 11, 2021), http://www.justsecurity.org/74138/incitement-timeline-year-of-trumps-actions-leading-to-the-attack-on-the-capitol.

[3] Lois Beckett, *Armed Protesters Demonstrate against Covid-19 Lockdown at Michigan Capitol*, The Guardian (Apr. 30, 2020), https://www.theguardian.com/us-news/2020/apr/30/michigan-protests-coronavirus-lockdown-armed-capitol.

[4] There follows a summary of Resolution H. RES. 24, 117th Congress (2021-2022) through which the House of Representatives accused President Donald Trump of having committed "high crimes and misdemeanors." Specifically, the resolution sets forth an article of impeachment stating that President Trump incited an insurrection against the government of the United States. The article states that:

- prior to the joint session of Congress held on January 6, 2021, to count the votes of the electoral college, President Trump repeatedly issued false statements asserting that the presidential election results were fraudulent and should not be accepted by the American people or certified by state or federal officials;
- shortly before the joint session commenced, President Trump reiterated false claims to a crowd near the White House and willfully made statements to the crowd that encouraged and foreseeably resulted in lawless action at the Capitol;
- members of the crowd, incited by President Trump, unlawfully breached and vandalized the Capitol and engaged in other violent, destructive, and seditious acts, including the killing of a law enforcement officer;
- President Trump's conduct on January 6, 2021, followed his prior efforts to subvert and obstruct the certification of the presidential election, which included a threatening phone call to the Secretary of State of Georgia on January 2, 2021;
- President Trump gravely endangered the security of the United States and its institutions of government, threatened the integrity of the democratic system, interfered with the peaceful transition of power, and imperiled a coequal branch of government; and
- by such conduct, President Trump warrants impeachment and trial, removal from office, and disqualification to hold U.S. office.

Cong. Rsch. Serv., H.Res.24 – Impeaching Donald John Trump, President of the United States, for High Crimes and Misdemeanors. Summary (2021). For a comparative analysis of impeachment procedures, also beyond the United States, see Tom Ginsburg, Aziz Z. Huq & David Landau, *The*

Comparative Constitutional Law of Presidential Impeachment, 88 U. Chi. L. Rev. 81 (2021).

[5] Gigliola Sacerdoti Mariani, Antonio Reposo, Mario Patrono, *Guida alla costituzione degli Stati Uniti – Duecento anni di storia, lingua e diritto* 105 (2nd ed. 1991).

[6] Hans L. Trefousse, *State of the Union – New York and The Civil War* 14 (2002).

[7] Tara Law, *What to Know about the U.S. Presidents Who've Been Impeached*, Time Online, Jan. 13, 2021, https://time.com/5552679/impeached-presidents/.

[8] On the word "impeachment" as used by the Philadelphia constituents, one can refer to the summary, which we give in translation below, by Sacerdoti Mariani et al., *supra* note 5, at 81, note 15. The origin of the institution of the impeachment can be found in English law: Thought up in the fourteenth century – as an instrument to be used by the House of Commons to accuse high officials of the realm for a whole raft of crimes and send them for trial to the House of Lords. It was in decline at the end of the eighteenth century. First from the historical and juridical point of view, the term has to be made clear linguistically: The verb "impeach" and the noun "impeachment," of French origin (cf. the modern French "empêcher" and "empêchement") mean, respectively, "to impede" and "impediment." In effect, the immediate consequence in the American impeachment process for the accused indicted by the House of Representatives (U.S. Const. art. I, § II, cl. 5), tried by the Senate (U.S. Const. art. I, § III, cl. 6) and found guilty (U.S. Const. art. I, § III, cl. 7) is to be immediately removed from office: He is "impeded," that is, from keeping a post of high responsibility, such as of President and Vice President.

[9] Donald Trump's legal defense complained, in the preliminary phase, that Trump could be tried by the impeachment process, and this was because a President could not be removed from office if he was no longer in office. The argument, though suggestive, is weak. The eventual conviction of a President, there can in fact follow, pursuant to U.S. Const. art. I, § III, cl. 7, aside from the removal from office – the main punishment – still more: Of "trial, sentencing and conviction pursuant to laws in force"; and thus, in this case, there can also be a further penalty consisting of being permanently banned from public office, including the office of President. This is the reason that explains the fact that a trial for impeachment of Trump took place even after the inauguration of the new President. In this way, Donald Trump remains a unique case of holding a double record: He is the only President to have been impeached twice; and the only President to have been tried by the Senate after he had returned to being a private citizen.

[10] Here, for the reader's convenience, is the complete text of Section III of the Fourteenth Amendment: "No person shall be a Senator or Representative in Congress, or Elector of President and Vice President, or hold any office, civil or military, under the United States or under any State, who,

having previously taken an oath as member of Congress, or as an officer of the United States, or as a member of any State legislature, or as executive or judicial officer of any State, to support the Constitution of the United States, shall have engaged in insurrection or rebellion against the same, or given aid or comfort to the enemies thereof. But Congress may, by a vote of two-thirds of each House, remove such disability." U.S. Const. amend XIV, § III.

[11] J. Wagstaffe, *Time to Reconsider the 14th Amendment for Trump's Role in the Insurrection*, Just Security (Feb. 11, 2021), https://www.justsecurity.org/74657/time-to-reconsider-the-14th-amendment-for-trumps-role-in-the-insurrection/.

Part Three
Some Potential Bolsters to Insert (or Restore) in the American Democratic System

13 The Fragility of American Democracy

We have then come to the fundamental question, that will in turn form the premise and starting point for further discussions. Now, the point to explain is this: How did it happen that someone – Donald Trump – was able to wield the role and powers of President of the United States for the entire term of office and was able, at the end of his term, to stand at the next election with the chance of being re-elected, despite the fact that originally there was no certainty as to the validity of his election to the presidency; and that he had been able to remain in office in spite of having – in terms of his accusers – twice, once in 2016 (the so-called Russiagate) the second time in 2019 (the so-called Ukraine affair), attempted to change the result of the election to the White House, and also notwithstanding two successive impeachment processes begun against him for facts that occurred on his presidential term; and also in spite of his having issued executive orders aimed at subverting the basic rule of American society and the very fundamental principle that inspirits many of the most important clauses of the Bill of Rights, that is the constitutive presence in America and of America of the most diverse ethnicities, the so-called melting-pot, to bring together in ordered co-existence around shared values; and finally despite that President having seriously risked undermining the principle by which democratic consent does not exist unless it is checked by means of ad hoc procedures and thus cannot be presumptive nor by acclamation. In plain English, the question to pose revolves around the reason why American democracy did not strongly repulse a President who proved able to lead a revolt against the major symbol of American democracy, or at least refused to thwart it with all the necessary energy.

The answer to this question is inevitably intertwined with the answer to another question: What can be done, in the domain of the interpretation and practice of existing law, so as to inject new anti-bodies into the American system of government able to avoid – as much as possible – that a new Trump appears on the horizon wreaking new and worse havoc on American democracy? Hans Kelsen, the greatest theorist of democracy of the twentieth century, stated that those who advocate democracy cannot let themselves be entangled in the fatal contradiction of resorting to dictatorship to save democracy. One must remain loyal to one's flag even when the ship is sinking.[1] We cannot but agree with him. Nevertheless, where necessary, dem-ocratically "sustainable" patches must be applied in order to avoid that the ship of democracy is shaken and, possibly, sunk by a future storm.

Now, having established that the greatest threats to democracy cannot but come, in the American system of government, from the person exercising the role of Chief Executive, the issue is to pinpoint moments or situations evincing the major criticality in this regard, and then to come forward with reasonable proposals as to how to eliminate them. However, we must never for one moment forget that the first defense of the institutions of democracy, in the United States as anywhere else where they are in force, is the routine duty of the citizens. It will certainly not be experts of constitutional law who will save democracy.

Before Approaching the Starting Line: An Indispensable Reliability Test

The federal Constitution, Article II, Section I, cl. 5, stipulates three requirements for eligibility to the Office of President of the United States: (a) being a "natural-born Citizen, or a Citizen of the United States"; (b) "to have attained to the age of 35 years"; and (c) "to have been fourteen years a resident within the United States." However, nothing, in the Constitution or in the federal or state legislation, sets down anything concerning the moral stature of candidates for the presidency.

The really strange thing is that, while any federal officials that the President nominates with the advice and consent of the Senate[2] is subject to severe scrutiny as to their moral fiber, not only professionally but also in their public life, to the contrary anyone standing for the highest-grade federal office is not subjected to any screening of this kind. A person can thus run, and even be the candidate designated by the national Convention of each party, in spite of having a blemished criminal record or of having been guilty of misconduct in public.

As a general rule, this is not a problem: Those offences can be inconsequential, and in fact in most cases they are. Some offences and wrongdoings, however, by their very nature preclude eligibility to the office of President or should undoubtedly do so.

In other words, in the American system of government, the President is given the task of leading the Federation, and this more so in moments of crisis. More and better: The President is entrusted with the task of leading the whole Western world, while his decisions have effects on the entire community of states and peoples. Therefore, the American people must be able to put the greatest faith in him and must be able to trust him. Consequently, as a matter of principle, nobody should be eligible to run for the presidency if they have faced criminal convictions for offences that render them unworthy of public trust; let alone become President.

On the other hand, the Constitution, at Article II, Section I, cl. 8, requires that the President-elect, before taking office, take the Oath or Affirmation to preserve, protect, and defend the Constitution "to the best of [his] ability." This means – among other things – that the President solemnly swears (or affirms), identifies himself intrinsically, with the fundamental values of the Constitution, including the Bill of Rights and the other constitutional amendments, as interpreted by the courts; and it is no accident that the Chief Justice of the Supreme Court swears in the President on his inauguration. Thus, someone cannot be deemed fit to take office as President if he has in any way (through writing, videos, or public debates) committed acts intended to subvert the economic, social, and political ordinances of the country or has flouted the Constitution.

To avoid this happening, it is necessary, at the level of federal standards or commonly accepted practice, that the parties affirm the rule that each candidate running for the presidency, regardless of which party he represents, submit to the national Committee the pertinent documents that should be made public. At the same time, each candidate – even before the race to designate the team of each party – is subjected by the national Committee to severe scrutiny to ascertain the real degree of his trustworthiness in terms of the presidential office and all that that office entails.

During the Term of Office

The Trump presidency in many ways constituted the "wind tunnel" of the American system of government. There came to the surface numerous functional problems warranting identification and correction in order to avoid that at the next U-curve – that will come sooner or later – American democracy might go off the rails and end up in a ditch. Let us look at these problems one by one.

On the Special Counsel Empowered with Investigating Irregularities in the Presidential Election

"We" – wrote Gaetano Salvemini – "cannot remain impartial. We can only be intellectually honest. Impartiality is a dream, probity is a duty." Correct, probity is a duty; the discharge of which may however be disrupted, delayed, and made difficult by several factors. For someone undertaking a judicial investigation, the disturbance might derive, for example, from testimonies that are false, reticent, contradictory, or retracted; otherwise, in certain cases from threats, more or less veiled, and, as it were, floating in the air, of being dismissed or the investigation being closed. All of these things are aimed at deflecting the investigation from uncovering the truth.

Something of the kind also happened, reading the Mueller Report, to the Special Counsel on Investigation charged with finding the true facts about the so-called Russiagate. Moreover, this was followed up also after the end of the investigation through a series of skillfully orchestrated acts, such as President Trump's use, between November 25 and December 20, 2020, of the power of granting presidential pardons *in articulo mortis*, to figures such as Paul J. Manaford Jr., Roger J. Stone, and Michael Flynn. The first two were accused by Special Counsel Mueller of obstruction of justice and false statements and subsequently convicted (of this and other offences) in courts of law; the third had previously collaborated then later retracted his statements made to the Special Counsel; all of them, in any case, were pardoned by the very President on whose behalf they had run the risk of making false testimonies, or – in the case of Flynn – of retraction "under counsel."[3]

This situation had a precise cause. Anne Milgram, with her customary candor, says it pure and simple: The cause lies in the fact that the pertinent regulations place the Special Counsel within the Department of Justice, headed by the Attorney General. Thus, the situation arises in which the President nominates the Attorney General, who, being head of the Department of Justice, is authorized also to supervise the actions of the Special Counsel.[4] Consequently, in a nutshell, the President under investigation has a thousand ways to condition the very investigation that is probing into his actions. This organizational arrangement – the Special Counsel on Investigation within the Department of Justice – is thus not fit to purpose.

No better is the other arrangement tried up to now, that of making the Special Counsel an independent agency. As the proof of facts has demonstrated, such an organizational structure risks transforming this office into an uncontrollable entity that is too powerful. The path to follow may perhaps be different from both the former and the latter ones that have preceded it.

Those who, more than anyone else, have an interest in knowing whether or not the election of the President was done in a proper manner, are "We the People." Now, "We the People" is reflected in

Congress: That is the (only) political institutional locus where seats representing the entire country are allocated.

It is precisely to Congress that the Constitution assigns the very delicate task of bringing a President to justice, and thus also any President whose election was irregular or illegal. To be exact, the drafting of the indictment is the task of the House of Representatives pursuant to Article II, Section IV, of the Constitution; the Senate, presided over by the Chief Justice of the Supreme Court, is responsible for the impeachment trial based on Article I, Section III, cl. 6, of the Constitution.

Thus – this is the route we are indicating – it is the House of Representatives, and nobody else, that should nominate the Special Counsel on the basis of a resolution concurred by two-thirds of the members, and again two-thirds can remove him from office for unworthiness or any other grave reason. The Special Counsel, who must operate supervised by the Homeland Security Committee, refers to the House his final report and all other relevant information.

This organizational solution has the merit of transferring the Special Counsel out of the sphere of presidential control, that is of the sphere of influence of the person under investigation, and into the circle of the House of Representatives: Which, of the two branches of Congress, is the one that better represents "We the People as a Whole." It also has another advantage, of keeping the Special Counsel under strict bipartisan democratic control.

On the Justice Department's Office of Legal Counsel

Starting in 2010, when Professor Bruce Ackerman, already well known in the academic world for having written in 2000 *The New Separation of Powers*,[5] published *Decline and Fall of the American Republic*,[6] there have interfaced, one contraposed to the other, two interpretations of the modus operandi of the Justice Department's Office of Legal Counsel (OLC).

One theory, indeed proposed by Ackerman himself, affirms the progressive weakening of the independence and of the consequent impartiality of this office that is tasked, among other things, with keeping the entirety of the President's decisions – regardless of being taken in relation to domestic or foreign policy – within the guide rails of legality. In other words, its task is to uphold the rule of law in the executive branch even before those decisions are eventually checked by courts. This office has become by now – according to Ackerman – hostage to the President to the point of confining itself to placing a legal "fig leaf" over his decisions. Sooner or later this will lead, warns Ackerman, to the transformation of the executive power into something arbitrary; and that the fanatic who, asserting that his election represents a "mandate" from the people for massive change," one day or another should take control of it will bring down American democracy.

The opposing interpretation, given notably by Trevor W. Morrison,[7] defends (or defended) to the hilt the OLC, which – according to Morrison – has always preserved intact over the years the essential characteristics of independence and integrity in dealing with the presidency, characteristics that somewhat form the "existential" backbone of the OLC. From this comes Morrison's conclusion that, thanks precisely to the OLC, the rule of law as pre-emptive cage hemming the President's activity has never ceased to function. Eric Posner, another distinguished scholar of constitutional theory, seems to side with Morrison and against Ackerman.[8]

This contraposition will drag on for some time to come. But, as we know, if it is true that everyone has their reasons, it is also true that not everyone's reasons are right. The arbiter that decides, in this kind of case, who is right and who is wrong is the reality of politics.

It is here, precisely in the political arena, that two facts have occurred. First, Donald Trump was elected as President in 2016. The second factor is what could be defined the "clock's memo for Trump." Just two days – on January 19, 2020 – before the first impeachment trial of Donald Trump (January 21, 2020), the OLC produced a "memo" arguing the invalidity of the authorization by the House of Representatives of an impeachment investigation against the President. This same memo was then included by Trump's attorneys in their defense file. Constitutional Law Professor Noah Feldman (Felix Frankfurter Professor of Law at Harvard Law School) comment-

ed with a brief note.[9] There, starting from the least partisan memos
that have followed one another, from those related to Watergate involving Nixon up to the just-mentioned pro-Trump memo, he casts a
suspicious shadow on the relations between the OLC and the presidency over the last 50 years. Ackerman was right: In his diagnosis
and in his prognosis.

The fact is that, considered in terms of the sheer balance of power,
the current relationship between the President and the OLC is not a
balanced one. There has thus been a consolidation over the years of a
full-fledged "chain of command": Which, starting from the President,
proceeds down through the U.S. Attorney General to the Assistant Attorney General, put in charge of the OLC, and from him it reaches the
OLC, that adapts to the situation. It is possible, as well as necessary,
to implement within the executive branch a mini-balancing of powers
between the Chief Executive and OLC, between politics and the law.

Precisely in order effectively to redress the derangement that has
steadily been burgeoning, Bruce Ackerman has stepped in again suggesting a possible solution, pointing out[10] that the OLC has long lost
the capability to assess arguments in line with judicial logic, that is,
to assess the two sides of an argument impartially, leading to making
decisions on the merit of the case. Ackerman urged the President (at
that time the President was Obama, who showed no sign of wanting
to follow up on the suggestion; but the appeal remains valid for any
subsequent President willing to approbate it) to transform by executive order the OLC into a quasi-judicial institution, analogous in its
modus operandi to the Executive Adjudications Division, abolished
by President Eisenhower in the 1950s.

Ackerman's solution is certainly feasible, but not necessarily the
best one. A decision taken by a President, that would presume to
remain valid for successive Presidents (but who would have all the
means to abrogate it), always generates a feeling of discomfort and
aversion in whoever might have to comply with it. Better to pursue
a different course. Precisely in order to effectively redress the derangement that has steadily been burgeoning, it seems preferable to
put in place a solution, apparently weaker but in reality stronger, able
to draw on a code of considerate practice. The outgoing President

asks the President-elect – this is our proposal – to confirm up to the mid-term the U.S. Attorney General in office; at that point the new President, unless he has compelling reasons no longer to endorse the Attorney General, may, after two years, reconfirm or relieve him from office. Should he reconfirm him, the U.S. Attorney General will step down from office, without the option of a new confirmation, at the following mid-term; should he relieve him, the new U.S. Attorney General may be reconfirmed by the President-elect until the mid-term, and so on.

The advantage of this solution is that it implements sharing the OLC between the "two Presidents," the outgoing and the elect. This can lead in turn to an impartial management of the office and from here to greater supervision over the legality of executive actions.[11]

Notes

[1] Carl Schmitt, Imperium. *Conversazione con Klaus Figge e Dieter Groh* (Corrado Badocco trans., Quodlibet 2015) (1971).

[2] "The President, by and with the Advice and Consent of the Senate… shall appoint Ambassadors, other public Ministers and Consuls, Judges of the supreme Court, and all other Officers of the United States, whose Appointments are not herein otherwise provided for, and which shall be established by Law." U.S. Const. art. II, § 2, cl. 2.

[3] In relation to the collection of heavy and continuous attempts at interfering with the activities of Special Counsel Mueller and his closest collaborators, see Andrew Weissmann, *Where Law Ends – Inside the Mueller Investigation* (2020).

[4] *Scenes from the Mueller Probe (with Anne Milgram & Andrew Weissmann)* (July 22, 2020), at https://podcasts.apple.com/ao/podcast/scenes-from-mueller-probe-anne-milgram-andrew-weissmann/id1265845136?i=1000485703665.

[5] Bruce Ackerman, *The New Separation of Powers*, 113 Harv. L. Rev. 633–729 (2000).

[6] Bruce Ackerman, *Decline and Fall of the American Republic* (2013).

[7] Trevor W. Morrison, *Constitutional Alarmism (Book Review of Bruce Ackerman, The Decline and Fall of the American Republic)*, 124 Harv. L. Rev. 1688 (2011).

[8] Eric Posner, *Deference to the Executive in the United States after 9/11: Congress, the Courts, and the Office of Legal Counsel*, 35 Harv. J. L. & Pub. Pol'y 213 (2012).

[9] Aruna Viswanatha, *Justice Department Independence? Not with Trump*, The Wall Street Journal (July 21, 2021), https://www.wsj.com/articles/justice-department-underscores-independence-from-white-hou se-11626910625.

[10] Bruce Ackerman, *Abolish the White House Counsel and Office of Legal Counsel, Too, We're at It*, Slategroup (Apr. 22, 2009), https://slate.com/news-and-politics/2009/04/abolish-the-white-house-counsel-and-the-of-fice-of-legal-counsel.html.

[11] An overview of the possible solutions, but that does not contain the one presented here, is provided by Adoree Kim, *The Partiality Norm: Systematic Deference in the Office of Legal Counsel*, 103 Cornell L. Rev. 783–791 (2018).

14 The President: Roi Soleil of the Executive Branch?

At this point, it is necessary to analyze presidential powers, or, rather, how Trump used these powers during his term. Such an analysis is aimed at suggesting some strategies that may help get presidential powers "back on track," that is, constrain them with a view to using them correctly.[1]

It is actually trivial to point up the continuous and growing centrality acquired by the President on the national political scene. Of the two theories that from time immemorial, we might say, have vied over the issue of the powers of the President, one maintains that the President of the United States holds the powers of head of State and of head of the executive power categorically and that those are the powers, limited, enumerated, and delegated, that the Article II of the Constitution vests in him,[2] or that Congress has temporarily delegated to him according to a law; and the contrary theory according to which the President, as well as holding the powers of head of the executive power enjoys the far wider and less specified powers of the head of State. Of the two, the prevailing theory is the one that assigns to the President also powers not vested in him by the Constitution but arising from his being the privileged interpreter of the permanent and unitary interests of the national community, in terms of their historical continuity and in the framework provided by the Constitution.

This way of acting and of seeing themselves of American Presidents, and markedly so of those Presidents after Nixon, we find lucidly foreseen by Theodore Roosevelt in his *Autobiography*,[3] where that President of the far past (1901–1909) observed that he "... declined to adopt the view that what was imperatively necessary for the Nation could not be done by the President unless he could find some specific authorization to do it." On the contrary, he remarked that his "... belief was that it was not only his right but his duty to do anything that the needs of the nation demand unless such an action was forbidden by the Constitution or by the laws." Those words would seem to foretell a parallelism between the principle of the *residuum* of powers, laid down in the favor of Congress in Article I, Section I, cl. 18, of the Constitution, and the powers of the Chief Executive: Who would seem to be authorized to wield any power not specifically proscribed by the "Higher Law" or by statutes, and that appears necessary in the national interest.

The reasons for this status of the President as primarily responsible for national policies, inasmuch as he is the guide and reference point for the country, a position assumed with increasingly conspicuously in the last 50 years and that successive Presidents over time have for their part emphasized by every possible means, have been examined by legal experts and political scientists and are by now very well known. The conclusion has now in fact been drawn, with which very few disagree, that it is not so much the literal text of the norms contained in Article II of the Constitution: The Take Care and the Presidential Oath Clauses, pertaining to the command of the army and to his authority in international affairs; nor of other norms that in any case regard the President, as instead the particular interpretation and application that has been made of it under the conditions of the ceaseless sequence of emergency situations of the most varied nature – from Watergate to the COVID-19 pandemic and including along the way the 9/11 attack and the 2007 financial crisis – that has allowed the President of the United States, that is to say the President of the most powerful country in the world, to prevail vis-à-vis other state powers. All this, while the United States, following the tragedy of the Twin Towers, has become, more than ever, a "state of national security." By consequence, the emphasis now rests on Presidential oath of "preserving, protecting and defending the United States Constitution."

This also has a second reason that echoes the dynamics of counterposed forces. This second reason lies in the growing radicalization of American politics, a polarization – the experts agree also concerning this – that is at the root of the decline in the practice of bipartisanship in Congress and the consequent decline in the role of Congress itself in the global system of government. This is the case both at the level of decline in the capacity to adopt legislation, and of the weakening or fading, in terms of extent and intensity, of the political control of Congress over the Executive.[4]

Such a situation, on the one hand, calls on the presidency to assume, with respect to Congress, a role of substitution in the field of legislation,[5] and this explains the fact that the range of presidential interventions has gradually extended into new and unexplored areas, that is, that there has been an amplification of the spaces deemed to pertain to the President's law-making remit; and, on the other hand, facilitates the almost undisturbed exercise of his constitutional powers. This has brought about the stark imbalance of powers favoring the President, that same imbalance – as we have said – that Bruce Ackerman already in 2000 had indicated as harbinger of serious dangers for American democracy.[6]

Notes

[1] Alexander Bolton & Sharece Thrower, *Legislative Capacity and Executive Unilateralism*, 60 Am. J. Pol. Sci. 649–663 (2016).

[2] *MacCulloch v. Maryland*, Wheat 4, 316, 4. Ed. 379; *Scott v. Stanford*, 60 U.S. 303, 19 How 401, 15 L. Ed. 691.

[3] Theodore Roosevelt, *An Autobiography* 308–309 (1913).

[4] Molly E. Reynolds, *Improving Congressional Capacity to Address Problems and Oversee the Executive Branch*, Brookings (Dec. 4, 2019), https:// www.brookings.edu/policy2020/bigideas/improving-congressional-capacity-to-address-problems-and-oversee-the-executive-branch/.

[5] Edward G. Carminese & Matthew Fowler, *The Temptation of Executive Authority: How Increased Polarization and Decline in Legislative Capacity Have Contributed to the Expansion of Presidential Power*, 24 Ind. J. Glob. Legal Stud. 369 (2017); see also Casey Burgat, *Crippled Congress = Expanded Executive Powers*, Legbranch.org (Feb. 13, 2018), https://www.legbranch. org/2018-2-13-crippled-congress-expanded-executive-powers/.

[6] Bruce Ackerman, *Abolish the White House Counsel and Office of Legal Counsel, Too, We're at It*, Slategroup 655 (Apr. 22, 2009), https://slate.com/news-and-politics/2009/04/abolish-the-white-house-counsel-and-the-office-of-legal-counsel.html.

15   Trump on the Chess Board of Power, a Game in Three "Moves"

Then, suddenly, in 2016, Donald Trump stepped onto the proscenium of American politics. "Asserting that his election represents a "mandate" from people for massive change" (cf. Ackerman's Prophecy), Trump attempted to succeed in a venture that no President had ever tried before him: Turning the Executive into a self-sufficient power independent of the other powers.

This endeavor, that would certainly have been carried very far forward had Trump been returned to the White House on January 20, 2021, and that equally certainly whoever like Trump comes after Trump could not help but put into practice, hinges on three complementary and convergent "moves" aimed at a single aim: To turn the presidency into an unchecked, uncontrolled power.

The First "Move"

The first "move" pertained to the independent agencies. We know that, around the President, there exists an executive structure that can be described as a pattern of concentric circles. In the first circle are the closest collaborators of the President, who comprise the Executive Office. The second circle is made up of the Departments, headed by Secretaries, nominated and revoked by the President. In the outermost circle are the independent agencies and in particular the Independent Regulatory Commissions. Trump's intent was in fact to bring into the sphere of the President's control these structures as well, thereby effacing their distinctively independent character. Trump achieved some results in his plan.

In *Seila Law LLC v. Consumer Financial Protection Bureau*,[1] the Supreme Court took for granted the solution to the issue it had been called to resolve, that is that "Article II vests the entire executive power in the President alone." On this premise, the Court ruled, in principle, the unconstitutionality of the law restricting the President's right to remove "at will" the director of an independent agency protected from at-will termination and removable by the President only in case of "inefficiency, neglect of duty, or malfeasance in office." This applied to an independent agency led by a single director and vested with significant executive power.

Nevertheless, this "precedent" did not give sufficient assurance of soundness. A confirmation was required, that Trump needed with the goal of controlling this vast galaxy of Agencies through the power to remove their leaders ("You're fired"), that he had frequently applied in a state of legal limbo. Such confirmation was meant to arrive with a ruling of the Supreme Court for which Trump had been waiting for a couple of years, the *Collins v. Mnuchin* decision.[2] Then, finally, the decision arrived. In *Collins v. Yellen* (originally *Collins v. Mnuchin*), the Court had to judge on the constitutional legitimacy of the law setting up the Federal Housing Financial Agency, an independent Agency headed by a director who could be removed by the President before the termination of his mandate only by "for-cause" removal. In this ruling, the Court concluded – these are the words of Justice Alito, who drafted the ruling – that "[t]he Constitution prohibits even "modest restrictions" on the President's power to remove the head of an agency with a single top officer." Only, the Collins decision arrived on June 23, 2021. For Trump, this was too late.

If, however, the analysis of this point does not end here, this is because after Trump can come another Trump, or even Trump himself. The remark we can thus make is that this jurisprudence, that indulges the President too much, is weak, as well as dangerous. Let us see why, and how it can be remedied.

The two elements identified by the Court in *Seila* to judge on the constitutionality of the law regulating an independent agency were, first, the fact that at the head of the agency there is a single director or multiple commissioners, and, second element, that the Agency carries out a pre-eminently executive function, or rather a "quasi-legislative" or "quasi-judicial" one. Neither appear – singly nor the two taken together – too significant. The independent agencies have had from their origin a quasi-judicial function concerning relations between private entities, their conflicting interests and rights. Precisely, this reason for being explains why, in such situations, one wants to remove the sectors in which the single agencies are consulted from the conditioning influence of short-term politics and from control by the parties: Which would inevitably end up "supporting" one side or the other.

The question of the validity of the law that, removing the independent agency from under the control of the Chief Executive, "de-presidentializes" it can solely depend on the opinion of whether the interests and rights at stake in "that" sector have or do not have such importance as to be placed under strict dependence of the Executive. This opinion, underpinning the laws setting up each independent agency, poses a political question that, as such, can certainly not be answered in a court of law.

The only body qualified to decide in this regard is (and cannot but be) Congress, since it adopted the law itself. Let us think about this. In the United States, despite his separateness from Congress, the President wields enormous influence over the legislative power. He wields such influence in part by his power, vested in him by the Constitution, to initiate legislative measures through messages addressing the Houses, and also by the fact that through the veto power, the President can stop legislation approved by the Congress becoming law, and in part through the members of his party sitting in the legislative branch. In this way, many of the draft bills examined by Congress originate from the executive departments. This continuous conversation between Congress and President concerning legislation provides the two Houses with all the instruments for information and debate enabling it to fulfil their proper function. This holds true in general, but in particular in the case of laws that set up and organize the independent agencies. This means that Congress knows and is able every time to assess the President's opinion on the role and importance of the agency being founded.

Thus if Congress, perfectly aware of the view of the Executive, decides to write into law that the director of an agency cannot be removed from office except under the conditions precisely indicated in the articles of the law and not instead at the President's discretion, this means that it has resolved, in one way and not in the contrary way, the fundamental question of whether or not the agency is to be deemed under the control of the Executive. Moreover, and more decidedly still, the Supreme Court itself had ruled on this in *Humphrey's Executors v. United States*,[3] where it decided that the President's power of removal of officers from office was to be deemed limited to executive departments, given that the independent regulatory commissions are "ancillary" to the legislative and judiciary branches.

The Second "Move"

A second "move" by Trump to try to render the Executive a self-sufficient power independent of the other powers lay in governing by means able to elude the control of Congress.[4] One instrument he used more than any other to this end was the executive order.

The federal Constitution does not provide for, let alone regulate, executive orders as a form of legislation. The interventions of the President in the legislative domain – pursuant to the Constitution – come down to three: When he resorts to his veto power, based on Article II, Section III, cl. 1, that is a presidential power in the technical sense, enabling him to weigh in on the legislative work of Congress; when, based on the power vested in him by Article II, Section III, cl. 1, he recommends "to their Consideration such Measures as he shall judge necessary and expedient"; and, per Article II, Section III, cl. 1, when he uses the powers he deem necessary to "take care that the laws be faithfully executed."

It can thus be affirmed that executive orders are one of the great "black holes" of the American Constitution, a "black hole" into which – furthermore – is likely to be lost the accountability of the President toward Congress and toward "We the People." The point is that the executive orders, precisely because they are not provided for, eschew any kind of congressional control. As a matter of fact, starting with George Washington and all the way down to Joe Biden, all the American Presidents have made more or less wide use of executive orders as tools to step in domestic and foreign policy.

Painstakingly, the Supreme Court tried, through the famous judgement in *Youngstown Sheet & Tube Co. v. Sawyer,*[5] to fill in at least one aspect of that "black hole," trying to shape a test as to its validity, that is to establish when an executive order can be deemed compliant with the Constitution, and when not. According to the Supreme Court, executive orders are legitimate only in two cases: Where they are connected to one or the other norms of Article II of the Constitutions, that vests specific powers in the President, or when they are based in a law of Congress that specifically delegates the President to intervene in the legislative domain, except those matters where the powers of Congress were exclusive and not subject to delegation.[6] Justice Jackson, in turn, added a new chapter to this history when, in his (widely cited) concurring opinion, he came to accept as legitimate those executive orders enacted by the President due to the "inertia, indifference or quiescence" of Congress, in terms of not legislating when instead there was a clear need to do so.

Put to the test of experience, the commendable endeavor of the Court in *Youngstown* to stem the use of the executive orders has not achieved, for cumulative reasons, its desired effects.

In the first place, the courts have steadily stopped making use of the "reasonableness review" conducted on the basis of the Due Process Clause of the Fifth Amendment; a scrutiny that made it possible, in the event of a restriction of the right to life, liberty, or property, to ascertain whether the law of Congress or the act of the Executive were, or were not, "reasonable." This kind of review, without doubt robust, has been replaced by the more deferential test consisting of ascertaining whether the order under examination has or has not a

"reasonable basis," in other words whether it is reasonably linked to
a legitimate governmental aim.[7] A test concerning the content of an
order – its "reasonableness" – has been replaced by a test that could
be termed "relational": It is enough that the act has a link with one of
the powers vested in the President by the Constitution.[8]

In second place, in order to weaken the bulwark constructed by
Youngstown against the use of executive orders, the idea came that
the authorization of Congress to the President to intervene in the
legislative domain could be deduced, absent explicit delegation, from
the "general tenor of congressional legislation over the years." Such
legislation indicates, or does not to exclude, the intention to vest in
the President a "broad discretion" to intervene in foreign affairs for
reasons of national security.[9]

In third place, working in the same direction is the prevailing
conviction that the interpretation of the will of Congress to authorize
the President's legislative intervention be adduced from the executive
order itself avowedly based on the law and not vice versa by deduc-
ing the validity of the executive order from the interpretation of the
authorizing law.[10]

In fourth place, there is the ingrained habit of the courts to de-
fer to the Executive on the ground that they do not have the skills
or relevant background information to make decisions on essentially
political matters. In particular, the Supreme Court, as all common
law jurisdictions, had been strongly reluctant to hear cases involving
national security, since these matters were traditionally regarded as
strictly within the confines of the Executive. Even after 9/11 and the
practice of extraordinary renditions, the habit of the courts to tiptoe
in the Executive domain persists to put up a fierce resistance.

The consequence of all this is that over nearly 250 years of the
life of the United States, only once, in *Youngstown Sheet & Tube Co.
v. Sawyer*,[11] has the Supreme Court rejected an executive order of the
President, or rather twice, having to add the posthumous rejection
of the executive orders with which Franklin D. Roosevelt had authorized the ordered relocation of Japanese Americans in internment
camps, overturned "now for then" by the Court in *Trump v. Hawaii*,
referring to the *Korematsu v. United States* ruling: "*Korematsu* was

gravely wrong the day it was decided, has been overruled in the court of history, and – to be clear – has no place in law under the Constitution." There have also been two or three other executive orders pronounced invalid consequent on the declared invalidity of the laws on which they were based.[12] We have already said that the use of the executive orders is of course not confined to Trump. All Presidents, including Obama, have had no alternative other than to resort to executive orders, particularly when they have not enjoyed the majority support in the Senate.

Trump, simply put, has been able to deftly exploit – as some of his predecessors – what are the major loopholes in the system: The lack of political (congressional) control over the executive orders; and the relinquishment by the courts, and especially the Supreme Court, to undertake a "reasonableness review" of the executive actions for fear of hindering the political decisions of the President; and Trump has done this, overturning by means of executive orders crucial sectors of American policies: Climate, education, health care, immigration, and oversight of the media. Nothing new, so far.

However, the use made by Donald Trump of (some) executive orders was not just a means to circumvent the ordinary legislative procedure; rather, Trump aimed at sidestepping the rule of law, mischievously invoking the *raison d'état* (that is, national security) as a trick – or, better, as a strategy – to push Congress and, at the same time, excluding courts' review, as demonstrated from his request of "defense funds" to build the U.S.-Mexico wall, as well as by the very controversial case of the travel ban/Refugee Admission Program. This specific misuse of executive orders can be identified as uniquely "Trumpian."

This situation, that risks irreparably compromising the equilibrium between government institutions, and that risks moreover obfuscating the decisions taken by the established powers in the eyes of public opinion, is anything but easy to restrain. We, for our part, can only do one thing and that is to sound an alarm. Government decrees (in the United States, President's executive orders) stand as a manner of legislative intervention that is potentially very dangerous for democracy, because – against the background of a latent shift toward a highly personal and authoritarian wielding of power, and where "animal spirits" are resurfacing and we are witnessing the shameless stirring of people by one claiming to assert the law of might – it constitutes the main tool for forfeiture of law-making power from the hands of the representative assembly, high-jacked into the hands of a charismatic, plebiscite leader.

The Third "Move"

Trump's third "move" to disengage – as much as possible "under the current Constitution" – the presidency from the network put in place by the legal system of checks over the actions of the Executive, is to be found in the appointment of justice of federal courts of appeals and, most of all, of the Supreme Court, a body that has the unique and invaluable privilege to "say" what the Constitution says. From this perspective, the judicial appointments decided by Trump have in common a specific feature. And this is not because Trump decided to appoint people whose shared his approach on some sensitive issues, such as homosexuality, women rights, sexual violence, reproductive rights, disabilities, environmental matters; and not even because he restricted the choice of Supreme Court justices to those who embrace the judicial philosophy of originalism, despite the fact that it is certainly the core of judicial philosophy of all three of Trump's judicial nominees. Actually, each President, every time that, during his mandate, one or more seats in federal courts on in the Supreme Court are vacant due to death or resignation, appoints – after advice and consent of the Senate – someone who shares his political vision. The politicized judicial appointments have long been a problem in the American constitutional system, not certainly created by Trump. From the other perspective, the judicial philosophy of originalism is an ideological pillar of the American conservative legal movement. Thus, it is perfectly logical that Trump – as other Presidents before him – preferred this approach to make his choice. Nothing new until this point. What instead characterized specifically Trump's choice on Supreme Court justices is their view on the role and powers of presidency. And this approach was aimed at obtaining a (more consistent) imbalance among the three branches in favor of the Executive.

Let us consider, to demonstrate this, his ideas regarding the balance among the three branches of the federal government as expressed, first at their nomination or at the hearing stage before the Senate, of the justices who can be deemed the most "decisive" ones nominated by Trump: Neomi Rao, Neil Gorsuch, Brett Kavanaugh and Amy Coney Barrett.

The choice of Neomi Rao, nominated by Trump to the D.C. Circuit Court of Appeals, that plays a crucial role in the judicial system of the United States, immediately provoked strong dissent. "People for the American Way," in opposing the nomination, wrote a letter to the members of the Senate Judiciary Committee denouncing the fact that, among other things, "[s]he also has extreme views on presidential power that would disrupt the careful balance established by the Constitution and effectively place the president above the law." In effect, there are many passages, in the writings of Rao, where she depicts the President as undisputed head of the entire executive sphere, as the one who has in the arsenal of his powers all the means to minister unhindered to the general interest of the United States and to preserve, protect, and defend its Constitution.

In *The Administrative State and the Structure of the Constitution*,[13] Neomi Rao proposed to eliminate, through some adjustments, the "independence" of those agencies that are precisely called "independent agencies": By Congress vesting in those agencies, through delegation of powers, a far more restricted measure of discretion compared to what the agencies normally enjoy; and recognizing the power vested in the President to dictate to the agencies – within the minimum discretionary space provided to each agency – the guidelines of their operations, as well as his having the right to remove from office the director (or directors) in charge of them.[14] Consequently, the presidency would finally have ascendancy over the entire executive sphere, of which the agencies would become full-fledged parts.

Yet, in an article written in 2009, Justice Rao went even further, theorizing the possibility, or rather the duty of the President – as *ex-*

trema ratio – to go beyond formal law and beyond the very rulings of
the courts if the national interest required it.[15]

In terms of the "constitutional" thoughts of Justice Rao, the three
judges nominated by Donald Trump to the Supreme Court – Neil
Gorsuch, Brett Kavanaugh, and Amy Coney Barrett – during his
term in office, are certainly on the same level. They too, in fact, have
cast the presidency in an image that is the exact reverse – broad,
pre-eminent, and in a certain sense "fluid" – compared to the highly restrictive concept delivered by the Chief Justice of the Supreme
Court William H. Taft in his treatise *Our Chief Magistrate and his
Powers*[16]: When he discusses his exact view of the functions of the
Executive according to his conception being that "the President can
exercise no power which cannot be fairly and reasonably traced to
some specific grant of power or just implied and included within such
express grant as proper and necessary to its exercise" and that such
specific grant must be contained in the federal Constitution or in an
act of Congress approving its execution.

Before discussing Justice Neil Gorsuch, it would be appropriate to open (and immediately afterwards close) a parenthesis. It
has been argued, regarding his nomination to justice of the Supreme Court by Trump, that it was a "stolen seat." In effect, that
seat should have gone to Merrick Garland, designated by Barack
Obama in the last year of his presidency (on March 16, 2016). The
leaders of the Republican party, the majority party in the Senate at
the time, with Mitch McConnell heading them, decided to post-
pone the procedure of advice and consent until after the election of
the new President.

Acting in this way led to two consequences. The first was to hand
over to the voters not only the election of the presidential team but in
effect also the nomination of the new Supreme Court justice: Who,
on Trump's election, was no longer to be Merrick Garland, but instead Neil Gorsuch. The second consequence, far graver than the
first, was that the nomination of Neil Gorsuch marked one of the
great "turning points" in American politics: To be exact, it marked
the official disruption at institutional level of the bipartisan mood
Between the two parties, the expression and result of that modera-

tion and of that attitude open to compromise that the "spirit" of the Constitution of the United States calls for.

On the practical level, this approach should have prompted in Donald Trump, just as any other President when in a similar situation, a gesture of fair play by nominating the candidate already chosen by his predecessor; and Trump might have done this, had the Attorney General informed him of the fact that the President represents the entire Nation, and as such is presumably impartial between the political parties, and had the Attorney General also pointed out to him (as he should have done) that the oath to defend the Constitution, that the President swears on taking office, does not concern only the formal rules contained in the Constitution but equally the exhortation to staunch collaboration among the institutional bodies, that sums up its "spirit."

Let us now return, closing this parenthesis, to Justice Neil Gorsuch's thoughts about the executive power. One of the central issues of his activity as judge at the Court of Appeals for the Tenth Circuit has concerned the status of independent agencies. Gorsuch's critique is aimed directly at the delegation of powers by Congress, that is, at the very life source of the independent agencies. We know that the Supreme Court, in the case of *Yakus v. United States*,[17] upheld the faculty of delegation by Congress with the specification that it should indicate specifically the field in which the administrator must act in order to eventually determine if such actions were within the law. Consequently, according to Gorsuch, this has created within the system of government an immense area – occupied by the Independent Regulatory Commissions – where there have accumulated legislative, executive, and judiciary remits in open violation of a fundamental principle of the legislation, pointed out in the first three Articles of the separation of powers stipulated at the Philadelphia Convention. Gorsuch strongly criticizes this situation, considering the delegation of executive power contrary to the design of the Constitution, which establishes that "[a]ll legislative Powers herein granted shall be vested in a Congress of the United States, which shall consist of a Senate and House of Representatives." Clearly, should the Supreme Court approve (as it appears now ready to do) Justice Gorsuch's contention regarding the need to uphold the prohibition of delegation by Congress, a thesis that Gorsuch has recently reiterated in the dissenting opinion in the case of *Gundy v. United States*,[18] it would lead to the inclusion under the authority of the Chief Executive of the whole range of agencies.

The other point Justice Gorsuch has always vociferously maintained is the President's authority pertaining to national security and the management of emergency situations affecting the whole country. In line with the so-called sole organ doctrine, which claims to possess a certain eminence as some scholars, in the wake of Justice George Sutherland, erroneously allege it originated from a phrase of John Marshall,[19] Justice Gorsuch restores to the incontestable discretion of the President the assessment of the existence of a grave danger, either latent or imminent, and of situations involving national security or of an emergency situation, and also of the congruence and appropriateness of the measures to be taken to counter it.

The immediate and logical consequence of all of this is, all too clearly, to exclude in principle, or at best to reduce to a minimum, any political and/or judiciary control over the actions of the Executive. This means, yet again, disabling the functioning of the rule of law precisely pertaining to the decisions taken from the top of the executive branch.

Here a couple of things should be made clear. The four justices on whom we have shone the spotlight – adding here that Brett Kavanaugh and Amy Coney Barrett share the same ideas on the role and powers of the President, but for a few nuances, as those expressed by Neomi Rao and by Neil Gorsuch – are (this is out of any possible doubt) sincerely democratic and driven by the best intentions in advancing their ideas about the politics of constitutional law; quite the opposite, they are deeply convinced of the need to return to the orthodox Constitution, and that if their ideas prevail undoubtedly that would be the result. Yet, it must be equally clear that the institutional order that they envisage, should it garner widespread consent, can have no other effect than to put in the pipeline the theoretical framework legitimating an uncontrolled government under a possible future autocrat.

How can we reasonably have a conversation about the relations between the President and the Supreme Court? We can – perhaps – do it through the Senate. In this regard, the Constitution stipulates, at Article II, Section II, cl. 2, that the President "shall nominate, and by and with the Advice and Consent of the Senate, appoint ... Judges of the supreme Court." Our work states two things. First, that the President has in this respect unlimited power of designation, in the sense that the Senate cannot at all impose their own choice on the President. The second thing this analysis states – which for us is the only pertinent issue – is that the power of "nomination" and "appointment," while pertaining to the President, is vice versa limited by the need for each of his choices to be approved by the Senate.

The question is: What exactly does control by the Senate involve, that seems particularly to vex the justices of the Supreme Court so much? Certainly not the fact, perfectly natural and accepted, that the President, on there being a vacancy (created by death, resignation, or removal through impeachment) of a seat at the Supreme Court, should want to nominate those close to his "political" views, broadly speaking. No, the control in the hands of the Senate does not concern this point. Rather, it regards – apart from the moral stature of the candidates and their balance evinced in their judgements and in their mindset – the need, for example, that inside the Court, there remains preserved a "minimum" of balance between the two national parties, in the sense that the candidate chosen by the President should not nullify the presence of judges of different "political" orientation.

This is what for us now is of major importance. In fact, an imbalance would come about not only when representation inside the Court of one of the two parties were lacking, but likewise in the case – not examined by the Senate so far – that the nomination of one or more judges by the President has the effect of giving greater weight to those judges who advocate theories that can shatter the apparently miraculous system of crossed checks and balances between government powers constituting the true pillar of the American Constitution. Here, in this imbalance inside the system consequent on an asymmetry inside the Court, might be lurking the precondition – on the level of constitutional theory – for a slide from democracy toward authoritarianism. This seems all the more real, considering on one hand that the Supreme Court justices – who, it is well to remember, have been nine in number since as far back as 1869 – are life-time appointments and, in the words of a popular saying, "a member of the Supreme Court never resigns and only rarely dies," and on the other considering – without going too far in stating this – that the Constitution "lives" as the Supreme Court interprets it.

Notes

[1] 591 U.S. ___ (2020).

[2] 594 U.S. ___ (2020).

[3] *Humphrey's Executors v. United States*, 295 U.S. 602 (1935).

[4] Regarding this aspect of the presidency of Donald Trump some scholars refer to it as "unilateral" or "administrative" presidency. See Frank J. Thompson et al., *Trump, the Administrative Presidency and Federalism* (2020).

[5] 343 U.S. 579 (1952).

[6] *Schechter Poultry Corp. v. United States*, 295 U.S. 495 (1935).

[7] See Federal Judicial Center, *Judicial Review of Executive Orders*, https:/www.fjc.gov/history/administration/judicial-review-executive-orders.

[8] It should be noted that "proportionality" and "reasonableness" are concepts that common law jurisdictions are fully aware off. The early Canadian cases under their Charter of Rights developed a test based on proportionality that has been applied in New Zealand under the New Zealand Bill of Rights Act (NZBORA). The U.K. Supreme Court has also adopted the concept of proportionality when considering the protection of rights under the European Convention on Human Rights. Lord Sumption discusses this in full in the well-known case *Bank Mellat (appellant) v. Her Majesty's Treasury (Respondent)* (2013) UKSC 38 & (2013) UKSC 39.

[9] *Dames & Moore v. Regan*, 453 U.S. 654 (1981).

[10] Erica Newland, *Executive Orders in Courts*, 124 Yale L.J. 2079 (2015).

[11] *Youngstown Sheet & Tube Co. v. Sawyer*, 343 U.S. 579 (1952).

[12] Milligan, 71 U.S. (4 Wall.) 2; *Panama Refining Co. v. Ryan*, 293 U.S. 388, 55 S. Ct. 241, 79 L. Ed. 446 (1935); *Schechter Poultry Corp. v. United States*, 295 U.S. 495 (1935).

[13] Neomi Rao, *The Administrative State and the Structure of the Constitution*, Heritage Foundation (June 18, 2018), https://www.heritage.org/the-constitution/report/the-administrative-state-and-the-structure-the-constitution.

[14] Neomi Rao, *Removal, Necessary and Sufficient for Presidential Control*, 65 Ala. L. Rev. 1205 (2014).

[15] Neomi Rao, *The President's Sphere of Action*, 45 Willamette L. Rev. 527 (2009).

[16] William H. Taft, *Our Chief Magistrate and His Powers* (1916).

[17] 321 U.S. 414 (1944).

[18] 588 U.S. ____ (2019).

[19] *United States v. Curtiss-Wright Corporation*, 299 U.S. 304, 320 (1936) (Sutherland J.). See Louis Fisher, *Presidential Power in National Security. A Guide to the President-Elect*, 39 Pres. St. Q. 347, 358 (2009).

Part Four
The Constitution, Interpretation of the Constitution, and Democracy

16 The Twenty-Second Amendment

The aim of the present work, as said at the beginning, is to study the tools available to the U.S. democracy in order to defend itself. Defend itself, it is well to make clear, not against attacks from outside nor against attacks from inside at the hands of, for example, Islamic terrorists, Marxist revolutionaries, or any other organized group of whatever nature is ready to storm the power in that country. When we say "defend itself," we mean a defense against situations deliberately created in order to paralyze the regular functioning of the system of government. To "defend itself," more precisely, means here from the danger of an "own-goal" by and within the institutions themselves.

Donald Trump, for example, has frequently declared his intention to run for President in the 2024 elections. In the declaration where he acknowledged Joe Biden's victory, he in fact addressed his supporters with the following phrase: "Our incredible journey is only just beginning"; and recently too, he has reiterated his intention. Let us thus suppose that Trump implements his intention. The question is: Can he do it, in terms of constitutional law? The Twenty-Second Amendment, interpreted literally, seems to say yes, he can; and nobody, until now, has shown any doubts in this regard. Nevertheless, some doubts, and not minor ones, might in fact arise.

From the day of his inauguration at the U.S. Capitol, the Constitution sets the term in office of the President at four years (Article I, Section I, cl. 1). The provision is ambiguous, as it does not clarify whether, after four years in office, the President can or cannot be re-elected, nor whether the possibility of being re-elected is limited or not. Due to the silence of the Constitution on this point, initially a practice was established that did not allow the President to be re-elected more than twice consecutively, even though there were cases of further re-elections. For example, Grover Cleveland won the popular vote in 1884, 1888, and 1892; though in 1888, he lost the electoral vote due to the electoral college.

However, it was the multiple re-elections of Franklin Delano Roosevelt (1932, 1936, 1940, and 1944), albeit justified because occurring during a long period of emergency, that served to confirm the doubts expressed by Jefferson at the Philadelphia Convention, that the absence from the Constitution of a prohibition of the possibility of unlimited re-elections could lead to a "life-long" presidency or indeed even to a hereditary arrangement.

As a result of such confusing situation, in 1947, Congress proposed, in accordance with Article V, a provision that intended to stipulate legally the limit of two consecutive elections: The Twenty-Second Amendment, on ratification by the Assembly of member States, was adopted on March 1, 1951.[1]

There is only one situation, in accordance with the Twenty-Second Amendment, in which a person may hold the office of President for more than eight years. This time limit does not apply in the case of a President elected twice who, in having held the office of Vice President, acts as President for the second two years of the mandate of the previous elected President in the case of the latter's death, resignation, removal from office following the impeachment process or other permanent impediments. In such cases "that" President can remain in office for 10 years (but no more than 10).[2]

However, this Amendment, in Section I, literally states: "No person shall be elected to the office of the President more than twice." Thus, to the letter, Section I of the Twenty-Second Amendment seems to allow a person, who has already been President once before, to hold the office of President won by re-election, also not consecutively. In other words, to the letter the Twenty-Second Amendment does not prevent any person who has been President once before from being elected a second time, also not consecutively. But we know that the letter of a provision does not always provide its interpreters with an incontrovertible reading. We know that at times, the logical interpretation prevails, leading to a reversal of the earlier, easier reading. This also holds in the present case. Let us see why.

It has been said and repeated for a remarkable number of times that the pattern of separate and balanced powers (with every power acting as counter-power and a system of government "conceived as one of mutual or interlocking constraints") should prevent authoritarian shifts in Washington. This is not the case. Democracy is the fruit of reason; conversely, the emotions, as with the great passions of strongly held ideologies, pushes toward, and feeds, authoritarianism. Some will say that the passage of the United States from democracy to authoritarian rule, from reason to unrestrained fervor in the political arena, is nothing but a thought experiment. Nevertheless, some variables susceptible to quantification appear alarming. The demographic shift underway in the United States advances inexorably. The consequent rise in the political temperature is a fact that is already tangible today. That a large part of the wealth of the country is concentrated in the hands of the few is in turn undeniable. The blend of these elements, each of which can constitute explicated a threat to democracy, could kindle the flames that are now smoldering under the ashes; rather it is likely that this should happen in the not-too-distant future, and even more likely if the anchor of democracy is not duly bolstered right now.

Now let us suppose that President Donald Trump, or anyone after Trump and like Trump, not having been able to obtain a second consecutive term of office, declares his intent to run for the presidency at the next election. This intent might be grounded on the fact that he alleges to have obtained the votes of the "real American people," whose values and interests he claims to embody and be ready to defend once again, having in the meantime maintained full and unchecked control over his party, sliding more and more toward extreme nationalism. It is easy to imagine how "that" President, or rather, "that" ex-President, would use Congress (having it under control, even if only by a few votes, or maybe even only the

Senate, or not having it under control but only by a handful of votes) in terms of exercising a hard and persistent obstacle to every bill introduced by the President in office. Clearly, the aim of the "defeated" President is, in this case, to debunk the President in office and, at the same time, to favor a slow but relentless decrease in political consensus for the party that supports this President. The purpose of this strategy is to pave the way for the "defeated" President's re-election. In other words, the "defeated" President prevents the President in office from carrying out his policies and, in this way, he leads electors to believe that his own political agenda is the only one to be trustworthy. Thus, it is easy to imagine that the "defeated" President would use the Constitution as an "oppositional" tool. And let us suppose – further, consequential hypothesis – that Congress, and notably the Senate, were to decide at that point to crank up to the maximum the powerful motor at their disposal, turning their attention to three crucial factors: "War power"; the allocation of necessary funds for the executive apparatus to continue functioning; and the "appointment" of the high level public officials that the President has the authority to nominate. We need to talk briefly about each of these three aspects.

The Use of the Armed Forces

A widely credited view, albeit a minority and strongly opposed, gives the President, as Commander-in-Chief, the widest powers to assess the preconditions and modalities for the use of armed forces.[3] A Congress, however, that wanted to reduce to a minimum the President's role in this field would need to exploit the powers conferred on it by the Constitution pursuant to Article I, Section VIII: "To declare war"; "to provide for the common defense"; "to grant letters of marque and reprisal"; "to raise and support armies"; "to make rules for the government and regulation of the land and naval forces"; "to provide for organizing, arming, and disciplining, the militia," and also "to make all laws which shall be necessary and proper for carrying into execution the foregoing powers," to make rules that the

Constitution explicitly enumerates as vested in Congress: "Coeffi-
cient Clause." Any Congress determined to act in such a way – with
unprecedented political cynicism – would be one step short of reducing the President to little more than the "First General and Admiral"
of the United States.[4]

The Allocation of Resources Necessary to Enable the Executive Apparatus to Function

Material means available are essential to the executive branch to carry out its functions. Here Kate Stith is right: "Money is the essential
oil of government."[5] On the other hand, the Constitution, Article I,
Section IX, cl. 7, ascribes to Congress the task of conferring on the
Executive, drawn from the Treasury, the means necessary to cover its
proper functioning: "No money shall be drawn from the Treasury,
but in consequence of appropriations made by law..." Thus, to obtain
the means it requires, the Administration applies every year to Congress as the natural source (even though in fact not the only source)
of procurement of financial resources. Congress, holding in its hands
the "power of the purse," thus possesses a powerful arm to make a
different life for the President.

It can do this in many ways, customizing the appropriations with
which Congress authorizes each time the executive use of public
funds. Congress – this is the usual and most effective way – can reduce, also considerably, the President's interpretative and applicative
discretionary powers with regard to legislation; and it can do so also
concerning laws of crucial importance in areas like foreign policy
and national security, that is, precisely in the most jealously guarded
domain of presidential powers. It is certainly not "nice" for Congress
to do this too extensively, for a thousand reasons of public order and
political ethics, but it can do it.[6]

Moreover, remaining in the field of national security and foreign
policy, Congress may – as it has done in the past – reject the application for funds made by the President to support, for example,
partners in counter-terrorism operations.[7]

So, for instance, Congress – interpreting common popular feelings – rejected, through the "Boland Amendment," that became part of the "Defense Appropriations Act" of 1983, President Ronald Reagan's application to dispose of the necessary funds to bankroll the *Contras* guerrillas in their armed conflict with the Sandinista government of Nicaragua, a policy that was unpopular in the United States. Faced with the Reagan Administration's attempt to get around the "Boland Amendment" by making use of funds coming from other countries or from private agencies, Congress engaged in a lengthy, protracted battle against this type of behavior "circumventing the law," potentially able to result in a "contempt of Congress." And Congress fought this battle both by means of public hearings and of two subsequent "Boland Amendments," one in 1985 and the other in 1989, both designed to make ever stricter the initial prohibition.[8]

Thus, in another example that we have already widely discussed, Congress refused President Donald Trump's demand for funds to build a wall on the entire border between the United States and Mexico. Here, digressing slightly, we can see that the Trump Administration has taken steps to erect around citizenship a full-fledged protective barrier that is very hard to penetrate. To be precise, Trump's policies have created a naturalization blockade; consequently, now would-like U.S. citizen could lose out of their chance to vote. The ruse of the Trump Administration to divert the funds from a debit entry, "snatched" from Congress in that way, to reroute them onto the "wall building" entry, met the very strong resistance by the majority of political forces present within Congress (thus not only among Democrats but also including some Republicans). Such a resistance (aided by the intervention of some federal district courts imposing permanent injunctions) was repeated with equal strenght, immediately afterwards, when faced by the declaration of a state of national emergency by Trump in a try to self-finance his project.[9]

Precisely in relation to the issue of a national emergency, that arose following the invasion of Iraq ordered by President George W. Bush after September 11, 2001, and the consequent issue of *appropriating* the funds necessary to pay for the invasion, Bruce Ackerman – with the best intentions – suggested that Congress review the whole question with a view to finding a readjustment of the power situation in regard to "limited war," that today sees the President with the upper hand, and consequently also of the parallel appropriation process, that Ackerman judged to be at the time "erratic and chaotic." To be able to do this, Ackerman suggested a format that he defined as "rules for limited war."[10]

A Congress firmly determined to stand in the President's way could follow his suggestion in short order.

Nominating the Highest Officials in the Executive Branch

The executive branch, like the other two branches, constitutes a mechanism whose operation is regulated in its essential features by the Constitution. Steering this mechanism is the President's duty. At its base is an army of men and women employed in its various sectors. Between the base – the army of employees at middle and low levels – and the summit, that is the Chief Executive, there are a few hundred people, senior officials, who help the President to successfully complete the tasks assigned to him. The selection of these high rank officials lies with the President, who however makes the nominations with advice and consent of the Senate, due to a very precise decision made by the founding fathers, the Framers of the Constitution (Article II, Section II, cl. 2). The role of the Senate in the confirmation process is thus delicate and strategic. Speaking abstractly, the Senate can veer in this field from one extreme to the other: From head-on confrontation to loyal collaboration with the President. Here, various factors come to play decisive roles. One of them, having not a secondary relevance, consists in the propensity of institutions – for example, the Senate – to assert its own identity by trying in every circumstance to augment its own standing compared one to the other: Of the Senate in terms of the President and vice versa. This explains, for example, the idea that has been taking root over the course of time within the Senate as an institution, that maintains that the responsibility of nominating high ranking officials should be shared with the

President on an equal footing and is not a responsibility that pertains to the President who however fulfils it with the involvement of the Senate. This explains furthermore the hardly deferential attitude of the Senate toward the President in the matter of appointments in the main administration.

A second factor coming into play here in influencing the shift from collaboration to conflict between Senate and President is the concern that individual senators have or can have for their electorate. In certain cases, such concerns can turn the confirmation process into an occasion to barter with the President.

A third factor, which started to come into play at least 20 years ago if not more, consists in the ever-increasing radicalization of American politics, which we have already discussed. This situation has changed the modus operandi of the Senate: From an institution operating according to the criterion of unanimous consent and collegiate decision-making to one operating according to party lines. The Senate, in other words, has become an extremely "partisan" institution.

It is precisely the sum of these three factors, and of the third in particular, that explains the growing hostility met by the President in the matter of the advice and consent of the Senate, notably in the case of a "divided government." This has been described as a veritable "obstacle course."[11]

In such a situation, there remains the very broad not to say almost boundless – even after a first reorganization of the matter decreed by the Presidential Appointment Efficiency and Streamlining Act 2011[12] – opportunity for the majority party to create great difficulties for an "opposition" President by means of relentless obstructionism in regard to the 516 names about whom the Senate has been consulted; so great is the opportunity that an increasing number of scholars and political observers are insisting on soliciting a reflection by the Senate on the need to drastically reduce the scope for filibustering, currently viable almost without any limits seeing that the cloture rule sets at 60 the number of Senators (out of a total number of 100) needed to block obstructionism in the Senate.[13]

Notes

[1] "No person shall be elected to the office of the President more than twice, and no person who has held the office of President, or acted as President, for more than two years of a term to which some other person was elected President shall be elected to the office of the President more than once." U.S. Const. amend. XXII, § 1. On the limits of presidential mandates in the United States but also from a comparative perspective, see Rosalind Dixon & David Landau, *Constitutional End Games: Making Presidential Term Limits Stick*, 71 Hastings L.J. 359 (2020).

[2] Tom Ginsburg, Aziz Z. Huq, David Landau, *The Law of Democratic Disqualification*, 111 Cal. L. Rev. (forthcoming 2023) (discussing the Twenty-Second Amendment and pointing out the weakness of courts in case Trump had won a second election).

[3] Memorandum from the Deputy Assistant Attorney General – Office of Legal Counsel, *The President's Constitutional Authority to Conduct Military Operations against Terrorists and Nations Supporting Them* (Sept. 25, 2001) (J.C. Yoo).

[4] Jules Lobel, *Conflicts between the Commander-in-Chief and Congress: Concurrent Power over the Conduct of War*, 69 Ohio St. L.J. 391, 392 (2008).

[5] Edwin Meese III, William Barr, Louis Fisher, Geoffrey P. Miller & Kate Stith, *The Appropriations Power and the Necessary and Proper Clause*, 68 Wash. U.L. Rev. 651 (1990).

[6] On the numerous problematic aspects of the Appropriations Power of Congress, see Barr, Fisher & Stith, *supra* note 5.

[7] See Fisher, *supra* note 5, at 634.

[8] Richard Sobel, *Contras Aid Fundamentals: Exploring the Intricacies and the Issues*, 110 P. S.Q. 287-306 (1995).

[9] Resolution 9844, Fed. Reg. 4949 (Feb. 15, 2019). The declaration of a state of national emergency is another of the big "black holes" of the American Constitution. It calls attention, admittedly implicitly, to U.S. Const. art. I, § 9, cl. 2, which discusses the suspension of habeas corpus, and therefore to the powers expressly attributed to Congress, but in reality, the phrasing of the provision is such as to the subject entitled to declare it. See Leonard Fisher, *Address at the Senate Committee on the Judiciary: Restoring the Rule of Law* (Sept. 16, 2008); Bruce Ackerman, *The Emergency Constitution*, 113 Yale L.J. 1029–1109 (2004).

[10] Bruce Ackerman, *Limited War and the Constitution: Iraq and the Crisis of Presidential Legality*, 109 Mich. L. Rev. 496 (2011).

[11] Robert Bendiner, *Obstacle Course on Capitol Hill* (1964); Burdett Loomis, *The Senate and Executive Branch Appointments: An Obstacle Course on Capitol Hill?*, Brookings (2021), https://www.brookings.edu/articles/the-senate-and-executive-branch-appointments-an-obstacle-course-on-capitol-hill/.

[12] Maeve P. Carey, Cong. Rsch. Serv., R41872, *Presidential Appointments, the Senate's Confirmation Process, and Changes* (2012).

[13] Molly E. Reynolds, *What Is the Senate Filibuster, and What Would It Take to Eliminate It?*, Brookings (Jan. 20, 2021), https://www.brookings.edu/policy2020/votervital/what-is-the-senate-filibuster-and-what-would-it-take-to-eliminate-it/.

17   Two Redlines and a Conclusion

A "pincer movement," carried out on these three fronts with relentless determination by a majority party (or minority by only a slight margin) in both Houses or at least in the Senate during the whole duration of Congress or even during only one of the two terms, would enact two interlaced consequences, both of which planned and intended. The first is the semi-paralysis of the executive branch and thus, in other words, the inefficacy of the state machine. Italian political scientist Giovanni Sartori[1] wisely comments that prolonged efficacy grants legitimacy, whereas in an evolving society, any legitimacy deteriorates in the case of prolonged inefficiency. The second consequence, closely tied to the first, is that the effectiveness of democracy would be undermined, as it depends decisively on the efficiency and capacity of the leadership.

Basic to this strategy, its declared motive, is the Latin saying "*Salus rei publicae suprema lex*," that is, public safety is the supreme law of a country. Democracy, in words, is not the target. On the contrary, the targets (in words) are the "enemies" of democracy; however, of a democracy that is very far from democracy that in the Western world (and in the United States in particular) goes by that name. Not, then, a system of government marked by the restriction of power and by rights, but a political regime in which – quite differently – a pivotal role is given to the centralization of power and national security.

This is a first red line of our argument, centered around the danger, that is anything but abstract, that under given conditions, there may occur (a hypothesis that is highly improbable but not at all impossible) a situation of continuous paralysis of government action.

The second red line regards the political system of the United States, where, just as in any political system, there is a constitutional principle that could be called "existential" in character. This principle, not stated explicitly in any norm, can be inferred from numerous provisions contained in the Constitution, and requires continuity in the government process. Rather, this – it can well be said – was the major concern of the Framers, if not actually the only one.

Let us take as an example the regulation, both constitutional and legislative, pertaining to the deputizing of the President in case of removal from office, or death, or due to physical or psychological ailment. The federal Constitution in this regard is concerned about two things. One is to act in such a way that the office of President endures, or better, that each presidency is occupied throughout the full term of four years. The other is that there should not be a power vacuum between one presidency and the next. Therefore the "Higher Law" ensures that, according to Article II, Section I, cl. 6, a Vice President is elected *in tandem* with the President, precisely in order that the former successfully carries through the Presidency as deputy in case of need; and furthermore, to the same end, lays down that "...Congress may by law provide for the Case of Removal, Death, Resignation or Inability, both of the President and Vice President, declaring what Officer shall then act as President..." until the ending on "noon on the twentieth day of January" of the fourth year of the presidency: Twentieth Amendment (1933), Section I, cl. 1, ratified by the Presidential Succession Act of 1947, that also defined the order of further deputies: After the Vice President come, in order, the President of the House of Representatives, then the pro tempore President of the Senate, followed by the Secretary of State. Thus, on the other hand, it is also the Twentieth Amendment, in this case too ratified by the Presidential Succession Act, that makes provisions to ensure the continuity of the presidency, regulating in the case that, by January 20, it has not been possible to elect a President.

Alongside this type of norm, there are others also contained in the federal Constitution that regard not the continuity of the bodies of government as such but rather specifically the continuity of their activities. For example, Article I, Section III, cl. 4 states that the vice-President as President of the Senate "shall have no vote," unless the assembly "be equally divided"; or that each House can be authorized to oblige absent members to take part in sessions when a quorum is required, which is the case in the exercise of the function attributed to each House as "Judge of the Elections, Returns and Qualifications of its own Members": Article I, Section V, cl. 1. And more examples of the same type can be found.

But it is above all the reasoning that the Framers placed as basic to the Constitution, that it should ensure, and in fact has until now ensured, the continuous and constant functioning of the system of government. The American Constitution rests on two essential principles, one static and the other dynamic. The static principle is that which divides power among different institutions and the purpose of dividing it thus is to preclude the descent into despotism. It thus is a principle that eminently defends liberty. The separation of powers, nevertheless, entailing three mutually independent "bodies" that might be at odds, risks plunging the system of government into paralysis. That which furnishes dynamism and keeps it constantly alive is then the principle of interference among the functions assigned to the three "bodies," an interference that prompts the need for consensus founded on compromise. This is precisely the mechanism intentionally arranged by the Framers to enable the system of government to work, at the same time guarding democracy from too many risks.

Now, we can return to the text of the Twenty-Second Amendment. If continuity of the functioning of the bodies of government is deemed the fundamental principle, from the organizational point of view, of the whole federal Constitution; and if on the other hand, there is actively present in the political arena an ex-President endowed with exceptional leadership charisma and who aspires to re-election after having failed by a few votes to be re-elected at the end of his first term, the Twenty-Second Amendment – interpreted literally – constitutes a virtual threat to democracy in the United States. A threat to be accepted as inevitable, if the first sentence of Section I of the Twenty-Second Amendment – "No person shall be

elected to the office of the President more than twice" – seems to recognize that election to the presidency twice, also not consecutively, is
the only possible reading.

Actually, the literal interpretation is only the first step in interpretation, which then proceeds with research and examination of the
reasons and purpose of the premises of the provision to be interpreted. From this point of view, the legislative history of the Twenty-Second Amendment[2] underscores that the primary concern, both of the
proponents and of all those who took part in the debate at the Senate
and at the House of Representatives, was (and was only) to establish
the rule prohibiting a third election consecutive on the previous two,
which too, on their part, were consecutive.

On the possibility of re-election that is not consecutive on the
first election, there is total silence. Now, this silence can be filled
in two ways: Either by reading to the letter the first sentence of the
Twenty-Second Amendment, thereby conceding the possibility of
the non-consecutive re-election of an ex-President (an interpretation
of the Twenty-Second Amendment that might also be called "zeal-
ous") or by precluding such a possibility. The alternative between
these two mutually conflicting interpretations: One which appears to
be in line with the pre-eminent constitutional principle of continuous
operation of the bodies of government and entails the prohibition of
non-consecutive re-election; and another which, opening a breach to
the risk of paralysis in the system of government, is in clear contrast
with that principle. Well, this alternative places before the interpreter
not a choice but a precise obligation: To reject the dangerous interpretation of the Twenty-Second Amendment, adopting the other we
suggested. Is it at all admissible that the American Constitution, a
bastion of democracy, a "rigid" Constitution enshrining the principles of freedom and of equality, should come to be interpreted in a
way that is (even only potentially) damaging to democracy?

In conclusion, we can affirm that the American Constitution
establishes, on the issue of the election of the President, a general
principle, but that it also drafts an exemption to this principle. The
general principle, enshrined clearly albeit implicitly in Article II,
Section I, cl. 1, states that the President is not re-electable except in

the case that – this is the exemption introduced in the Twenty-Second Amendment – the second election follows immediately on the first.

Notes

[1] Giovanni Sartori, *Elementi di teoria politica* 47 (1987).
[2] Stephen W. Stathis, *The Twenty-Second Amendment: A Practical Remedy or Partisan Manoeuvre?*, 7 Const. Comment. 65–72 (1990).

18   A More Comprehensive View

In order to avoid potential risk that American democracy veers (at least in a future) into authoritarism, by means of identifying the fissures and by proposing some remedies to fix them can prove useful, perhaps indispensable; but certainly not sufficient. The demographic shift underway in the United States will lead, by 2050 if the predictions are correct, to a toppling of the numerical majority of the white population of the oldest or earliest wave of immigration – the guardians of traditional values and holders from the very beginning of the major financial and political resources, as well as of the main tools of social control – by the mass of women and men of more recent immigration, belonging to different ethnic groups and cultures. Hence, this bolstering operation in terms of interpretation and application of certain norms (be they few or many) in the laws and the Constitution probably cannot be separated, if the aim is to maintain the existing level of democracy in the country, from profound constitutional, political, and social readjustments.

Thus, it will prove difficult for the rule of equal representation of the member States in the Senate to endure, it being probable that it – already somehow undermined due to the Seventeenth Amendment (1913) – will be replaced with another rule determining that the number of representatives in the Senate will be proportional to the number of inhabitants of each State. It is also possible that the traditional two-party system may be replaced over time by a system comprising multiple parties, better able to reflect the multicultural character that the United States will have reached at that phase of its ethnic development.

What in any case does seem predictable enough is that the scenario of strong social tensions that demographical upheaval could entail will not leave unscathed, in its specific substance, the "American dream." It is unlikely, in fact, that the idea in the United States might withstand – almost miraculously, by the will of Providence – that everyone can achieve, as long as they have the will and the tenacity, the social role, and economic standing congruent with their personal talents. The numerical reversal favoring the underprivileged will solicit a profound review of that "dream." If it is to survive as a communal myth bringing together the various ethnic and cultural groups present in the country, it will have to abate by means of redistributive equalization policies able to truly give everyone equal (or not too different) competitiveness in terms of economic and educational resources. Additionally, there should be policies supporting those who, despite all, cannot or do not know how to compete in the struggle for life.

The whole collection of policies that we might define as "curbing social tensions" would however entail the renunciation of that individualistic and liberalist ideology that has dominated and continues to dominate American politics.